15 days
of prayer with
BLESSED FRÉDÉRIC OZANAM

CHRISTIAN VERHEYDE

TRANSLATED BY JOHN E. RYBOLT, C.M.

D1258378

NEW CITY PRESS
of the Focolare
Hyde Park, NY

Published in the United States by New City Press
202 Comforter Blvd., Hyde Park, NY 12538
www.newcitypress.com
©2013 New City Press (English translation)

This book is a translation of *Prier 15 Jours Avec Frederik Ozanam*,
by Christian Verheyde, published by Nouvelle Cité, Bruyeres Le
Chatel, 2011.

© Nouvelle Cité 2011
Used by permission. All rights reserved.

Cover design by Durva Correia

A catalog record is available from the Library of Congress.

ISBN 978-1-56548-487-0

Biblical quotations in English, taken from New American Bible,
(NABRE); used by permission. All rights reserved.

Printed in the United States of America

15 days
of prayer with
BLESSED FRÉDÉRIC OZANAM

Bishop Rassas —
May God bless
your journey

Janne Haye

15 days
of prayer series

On a journey, it's good to have a guide. Even great saints took spiritual directors or confessors with them on their itineraries toward sanctity. Now you can be guided by the most influential spiritual figures of all time. The 15 Days of Prayer series introduces their deepest and most personal thoughts.

This popular series is perfect if you are looking for a gift, or if you want to be introduced to a particular guide and his or her spirituality. Each volume contains:

- ☙ A brief biography of the saint or spiritual leader
- ☙ A guide to creating a format for prayer or retreat
- ☙ Fifteen meditation sessions with focus points and reflection guides

Contents

Dedication

To Bruno Dardelet who gave me the idea for this book; I am sincerely grateful.

To my wife Geneviève, whose *hand, more delicate than mine,* has corrected these texts, and who is my silent, modest and indispensable inspiration.

To Frédéric Vanpouille, a young and responsible member of the Society, a dynamic and sincere activist.

We have to let providence act, but we also have to give providence a hand.

How to Use This Book

*A*n old Chinese proverb, or at least what I am able to recall of what is supposed to be an old Chinese proverb, goes something like this: "Even a journey of a thousand miles begins with a single step." When you think about it, the truth of the proverb is obvious. It is impossible to begin any project, let alone a journey, without taking the first step. I think it might also be true, although I cannot recall if another Chinese proverb says it, "that the first step is often the hardest." Or, as someone else once observed, "the distance between a thought and the corresponding action needed to implement the idea takes the most energy." I don't know who shared that perception with me but I am certain it was not an old Chinese master!

With this ancient proverbial wisdom, and the not-so-ancient wisdom of an unknown contemporary sage still fresh, we move from proverbs to presumptions. How do these relate to the task before us?

I am presuming that if you are reading this introduction it is because you are contemplating a journey. My presumption is that you are preparing for a spiritual journey and that you have taken at least some of the first steps necessary to prepare for this journey. I also presume, and please excuse me if I am making too many presumptions, that in your preparation for the spiritual journey you have determined that you need a guide. From deep within the recesses of your deepest self, there was something that called you to consider Saint Teresa as a potential companion. If my presumptions are correct, may I congratulate you on this decision? I think you have made a wise choice, a choice that can be confirmed by yet another source of wisdom, the wisdom that comes from practical experience.

Even an informal poll of experienced travelers will reveal a common opinion: it is very difficult to travel alone. Some might observe that it is even foolish. Still others may be even stronger in their opinion and go so far as to insist that it is necessary to have a guide, especially when you are traveling into uncharted waters and into territory that you have not yet experienced. I am of the personal opinion that a traveling companion is welcome under all circumstances. The thought of traveling alone, to some exciting destination without someone to share the journey with does not capture my imagination or channel my enthusiasm. However, with that being noted, what is simply a matter of preference on the normal journey becomes a matter of necessity when a person embarks on a spiritual journey.

The spiritual journey, which can be the most challenging of all journeys, is experienced best with a guide, a companion, or at the very least, a friend in whom you have placed your trust. This observation is not a preference or an opinion but rather an established spiritual necessity. All of the great saints with whom I am familiar had a spiritual director or a confessor who journeyed with them. Admittedly, at times the saints might well have traveled far beyond the experience of their guide and companion but more often than not they would return to their director and reflect on their experience. Understood in this sense, the director and companion provided a valuable contribution and necessary resource. When I was learning how to pray (a necessity for anyone who desires to be a full-time and public "religious person"), the community of men that I belong to gave me a great gift. Between my second and third year in college, I was given a one-year sabbatical, with all expenses paid and all of my personal needs met. This period of time was called novitiate. I was officially designated as a novice, a beginner in the spiritual journey, and

I was assigned a "master," a person who was willing to lead me. In addition to the master, I was provided with every imaginable book and any other resource that I could possibly need. Even with all that I was provided, I did not learn how to pray because of the books and the unlimited resources, rather it was the master, the companion who was the key to the experience.

One day, after about three months of reading, of quiet and solitude, and of practicing all of the methods and descriptions of prayer that were available to me, the master called. "Put away the books, forget the method, and just listen." We went into a room, became quiet, and tried to recall the presence of God, and then, the master simply prayed out loud and permitted me to listen to his prayer. As he prayed, he revealed his hopes, his dreams, his struggles, his successes, and most of all, his relationship with God. I discovered as I listened that his prayer was deeply intimate but most of all it was self-revealing. As I learned about him, I was led through his life experience to the place where God dwells. At that moment I was able to understand a little bit about what I was supposed to do if I really wanted to pray.

The dynamic of what happened when the master called, invited me to listen, and then revealed his innermost self to me as he communicated with God in prayer, was important.

It wasn't so much that the master was trying to reveal to me what needed to be said; he was not inviting me to pray with the same words that he used, but rather that he was trying to bring me to that place within myself where prayer becomes possible. That place, a place of intimacy and of self-awareness, was a necessary stop on the journey and it was a place that I needed to be led to. I could not have easily discovered it on my own.

The purpose of the volume that you hold in your hand is to lead you, over a period of fifteen days or, maybe more realistically, fifteen prayer periods, to a place where prayer is possible. If you already have a regular experience and practice of prayer, perhaps this volume can help lead you to a deeper place, a more intimate relationship with the Lord.

It is important to note that the purpose of this book is not to lead you to a better relationship with Saint Teresa, your spiritual companion. Although your companion will invite you to share some of her deepest and most intimate thoughts, your companion is doing so only to bring you to that place where God dwells. After all, the true measurement of all companions for the journey is that they bring you to the place where you need to be, and then they step back, out of the picture. A guide who brings you to the desired destination and then sticks around is a very unwelcome guest!

Many times I have found myself attracted to a particular idea or method for accomplishing a task, only to discover that what seemed to be inviting and helpful possessed too many details. All of my energy went to the mastery of the details and I soon lost my enthusiasm. In each instance, the book that seemed so promising ended up on my bookshelf, gathering dust. I can assure you, it is not our intention that this book end up in your bookcase, filled with promise, but unable to deliver.

There are three simple rules that need to be followed in order to use this book with a measure of satisfaction.

Place: It is important that you choose a place for reading that provides the necessary atmosphere for reflection and that does not allow for too many distractions. Whatever place you choose needs to be comfortable, have the necessary lighting, and, finally, have a sense of "welcoming" about it. You need to be able to look forward to the experience of the journey. Don't travel steerage if you know you will be more comfortable in first class and if the choice is realistic for you. On the other hand, if first class is a distraction and you feel more comfortable and more yourself in steerage, then it is in steerage that you belong.

My favorite place is an overstuffed and comfortable chair in my bedroom. There is a light over my shoulder, and the chair reclines if I feel a need to recline. Once in a while, I get lucky and the sun comes through my window and bathes the entire room in light. I have other options and other places that are available to me but this is the place that I prefer.

Time: Choose a time during the day when you are most alert and when you are most receptive to reflection, meditation, and prayer. The time that you choose is an essential component. If you are a morning person, for example, you should choose a time that is in the morning. If you are more alert in the afternoon, choose an afternoon time slot; and if evening is your preference, then by all means choose the evening. Try to avoid "peak" periods in your daily routine when you know that you might be disturbed. The time that you choose needs to be your time and needs to work for you.

It is also important that you choose how much time you will spend with your companion each day. For some it will be possible to set aside enough time in order to read and reflect on all the material that is offered for a given day. For others, it might not be possible to devote one time to the suggested material for the day, so the prayer period may need to be extended for two, three, or even more sessions. It is not important how long it takes you; it is only important that it works for you and that you remain committed to that which is possible.

For myself I have found that fifteen minutes in the early morning, while I am still in my robe and pajamas and before my morning coffee, and even before I prepare myself for the day, is the best time. No one expects to see me or to interact with me because I have not yet "announced" the fact that I am awake or even on the move. However, once someone hears me in the bathroom, then my window of opportunity is gone. It is therefore important to me that I use the time that I have identified when it is available to me.

Freedom: It may seem strange to suggest that freedom is the third necessary ingredient, but I have discovered that it is most important. By freedom I understand a certain "stance toward life," a "permission to be myself and to be gentle and understanding of who I am." I am constantly amazed at how the human person so easily sets himself or herself up for disappointment and perceived failure. We so easily make judgments about ourselves and our actions and our choices, and very often those judgments are negative, and not at all helpful.

For instance, what does it really matter if I have chosen a place and a time, and I have missed both the place and the time for three days in a row? What does it matter if I have chosen, in that twilight time before I am completely awake and still a little sleepy, to roll over and to sleep for fifteen minutes more?

Does it mean that I am not serious about the journey, that I really don't want to pray, that I am just fooling myself when I say that my prayer time is important to me? Perhaps, but I prefer to believe that it simply means that I am tired and I just wanted a little more sleep. It doesn't mean anything more than that. However, if I make it mean more than that, then I can become discouraged, frustrated, and put myself into a state where I might more easily give up. "What's the use? I might as well forget all about it."

The same sense of freedom applies to the reading and the praying of this text. If I do not find the introduction to each day helpful, I don't need to read it. If I find the questions for reflection at the end of the appointed day repetitive, then I should choose to close the book and go my own way. Even if I discover that the reflection offered for the day is not the one that I prefer and that the one for the next day seems more inviting, then by all means, go on to the one for the next day.

That's it! If you apply these simple rules to your journey you should receive the maximum benefit and you will soon find yourself at your destination. But be prepared to be surprised. If you have never been on a spiritual journey you should know that the "travel brochures" and the other descriptions that you might have heard are nothing compared to the real thing. There is so much more than you can imagine.

A final prayer of blessing suggests itself:

> Lord, catch me off guard today. Surprise me
> with some moment of
>   beauty or pain
> So that at least for the moment
> I may be startled into seeing that you
>   are here in all your splendor,
> Always and everywhere,
> Barely hidden,
> Beneath,
> Beyond,
> Within this life I breathe.

Frederick Buechner

Rev. Thomas M. Santa, CSsR
Liguori, Missouri

Foreword

When I joined the Society of St. Vincent de Paul in 1995, I knew little about its founder, Frédéric Ozanam (1813-1853). I wanted to deepen my knowledge of this man of faith who was the embodiment of charity. His 1,448 extant letters, written to friends or family, plus some works mentioned in the bibliography, have helped me in this. I am going to share my discoveries with you.

His parents were solid believers, devoted to the Sacred Scripture, and engaged in the life of the society of their time. They had fourteen children, of whom ten died young, and they directed their childhood and youth (Day 1).

Adolescence was difficult for Frédéric, beset with questions and doubts, but resolved through the wise advice of his professor, Abbé Noirot (Day 2).

The great love of his life, Amélie, stayed with him until his return to the Father. Jean-Jacques Ampère would write of her: "This hand of hers, that Ozanam said was more delicate than his, was strong enough to give him his final drink, and his last embrace" (Day 3).

The birth of their daughter was their greatest happiness (Day 4).

His friends counted on him greatly. Whether in Lyons or in Paris, he loved their company (Day 5).

Frédéric took an active part in the foundation in 1833 of the first Conference of Charity. This group brought together some students eager to grow in the love of the Lord by putting themselves in service to the poor. They were hoping for a world that would be more just and more generous (Day 6).

His letters allow us to learn about his life, his faith, and his determination to reconcile science and religion (Day 7).

However, the beginning of this new form of activity was difficult. Many attacks came from both outside and inside the organization and darkened these years. His "little work" would become one of the most important associations in the world. It is present on six continents and remains faithful to its two essential missions: home visits and prayer (Day 8).

One question obsessed him: the enormous gap between those who have much, even too much, and those with nothing. For him, "a struggle is inevitable." He agitated for Christians to become mediators between these two enemy forces (Day 9).

When he brought up the question of extreme poverty with young people of good families, he awaked the consciousness of Christians to become engaged in the service of the poor for the love of God (Day 10).

An address he gave to workers in Paris brings us into a meditation on the meaning of life (Day 11).

For Ozanam, teaching was a genuine vocation. Whether in Lyons or Paris, he imparted both his faith and his knowledge (Day 12).

The Church rarely places on its altars the merits of a committed laymen, married and father of a family. We rejoice and pray to Frédéric in our activities (Day 13).

His absolute confidence in Providence — this word occurs in many of his letters — moved him forward with assurance and peace. What a model for us! (Day 14).

A marvelous moment is the reading of his testament, written on his fortieth birthday. It is a long meditation by a brilliant intellectual at the difficult time of passage from this life. After revolting against his approaching death, he accepted the will of the Father (Day 15).

Historical Overview
Frédéric Ozanam
(1813-1853)

*O*n Friday, 22 August 1997, the day of the beatification of Frédéric Ozanam at Notre Dame of Paris, the Church, through John Paul II, "today confirms the choice of Christian life made by Frédéric Ozanam, along with the way that he chose. She says to him: Frédéric, your way has truly been the way of holiness."

In 1813 the end of the French Empire was at hand: Napoleon I abdicated on 6 April 1814. Romanticism began to influence French and European society, as Ozanam's writings show. Frédéric Ozanam was born on 23 April 1813 in Milan, the capital of the kingdom of Italy, which then belonged to the Empire. He was baptized on 13 May. His father had a varied life. In Year II of the Revolution (1793), he was a soldier and took part in the Italian campaign. After he left military service, he married in Lyons in 1800. He had two children in quick succession: Elizabeth (1801) and Alphonse

(1804). Since he had made some poor invest-
ments because of the continental blockade
against Napoleon, he moved to Italy without
his family. At first he was a traveling salesman,
and then he opened a small rooming house in
Milan. His wife and their two children joined
him in 1809. He gained his medical degree in
December 1810 at the age of thirty-nine, and
he then practiced medicine in Milan. After
Napoleon's defeat at Waterloo in 1815 the family moved back to Lyons in October 1816.

Frédéric was the fifth child of a family of
fourteen: five boys and nine girls. Eight of the
girls and two of the boys died in childhood.
The eldest, Elizabeth (called Elisa) died in 1820,
at age nineteen. By 1824, the family had been
reduced to three children: Alphonse (1804-88),
a physician and priest; Frédéric (1813-53); and
Charles (1824-90), another physician. The family lived modestly, but had sufficient means.
The father, a physician at the Hotel-Dieu of
Lyons, also had private clients. The mother
was a volunteer in an association of working
women, called La Veilleuse.

Frédéric was a brilliant student, and his
father wanted him to become an attorney.
During his last year of studies at the royal college (or secondary school), Fr. Noirot, his philosophy professor, helped the young Frédéric,
tormented by doubts, to keep the faith. Frédéric
was intellectually well endowed, with a strong

inclination toward literature. He learned classical and modern languages. His professor boasted that "his facility in writing Latin is extraordinary." When he graduated from secondary school in 1830, he spent a year clerking for an attorney. Since Lyons had no faculty of law, Frédéric, on 2 November 1831, took an eighteen-person carriage for Paris, where he arrived on Saturday, the sixth, to enroll in the Sorbonne. The uprising of the Lyonnais silk workers, the *canuts*, which broke out on 21 November 1831, was his first experience of the face-to-face encounter between the bourgeoisie and the proletariat. In three days, it resulted in about 169 dead and 403 wounded, plunging Frédéric into anxiety for his family.

He had a hard time getting used to Paris. André-Marie Ampère, a Lyonnais like him, took him under his protection and gave him hospitality. Since his legal studies gave him some liberty, Frédéric also took courses in the faculty of letters. He received his Doctorate in Laws in 1836, and Doctorate in Letters in 1839. In 1840, he also won first place in the competition for a teaching position in literature.

Ozanam was the promoter of the Lenten conferences at Notre Dame of Paris. From 1835, he secured Fr. Lacordaire as the preacher for these conferences. They still attract many Christians.

The traits of his character come to the fore after reading his 1,448 published letters:

- ☙ his unbreakable **faith**, after the doubts of his adolescence; his confidence in Providence;

- ☙ his **humility**, in the building up of the Society of St. Vincent de Paul. We read numerous times of "our little society," or "our little work";

- ☙ his **hope in the future**: for him the revolution of 1848 was an unexpected opportunity. He saw in it the temporal future of the Gospel as expressed in these three words: "Liberty, Equality, Fraternity!"

- ☙ his **love for the poor**: Ozanam had this to a degree that others rarely attained. Guided by the example of his parents, throughout his life he would visit the poor, even if he was quite ill. He would also give public witness to his love of justice and charity;

- ☙ his social **opinions** were quite advanced: Ozanam tried to mediate between those who had much or even too much, and those who had little or nothing. He often returned to this issue in nearly identical terms. He was truly obsessed by trying to reconcile science and religion, wealth and poverty, believers and unbelievers. Many of his texts demonstrate his stubborn zeal. He was a genuine apostle, burning "with the same desire to preach the truth and to save souls." At the time of the 1848 revolution, he sought Archbishop Affre's intervention to put an end to the fighting in the faubourg St.-Antoine. A stray bullet would strike down the archbishop of Paris;

ℭ his **friends** were indispensable for him: "I can never be without my friends." He joined a group of students in both Paris and Lyons with whom he kept up a regular correspondence. Friendship was the key word for him, whether for moments of happiness (the marriage of his friends), or of sorrow (the loss of a father or mother.) When he came to Paris, alone in the big city, he assembled a group of Lyonnais who lived and played together.

He practiced law only briefly, especially since he disliked this profession. Instead, his whole life evinced an interest in journalism: from age sixteen, he wrote in the *Abeille française*. He would write in several newspapers. In April 1848, he founded, with Frs. Maret and Lacordaire, *L'Ère nouvelle*. It was there that he developed his vision of society and

the world. He was a writer: besides his doc-
toral dissertation on Dante (1245-1321), other
works received prizes, such as this one from
the French Academy: *The Germans before
Christianity*; also *The Franciscan Poets in Italy
in the Thirteenth Century* (which, for Ampère,
was "a masterpiece of knowledge and grace");
the *Life of St. Eloi*; *Two Chancellors of England*; *A
Pilgrimage to the Land of the Cid* (1853), and others. He entered politics: moved by his friends
from Lyons, he ran for the first elections held
under the universal suffrage of 1848 (with eight
million voters). He received more than 15,000
votes, but he lost the election. He was, more
than anything else, a professor, a founder, and
a husband.

Professor

In July 1839, he received the appointment
of teaching commercial law in Lyons. As
a professor *agrégé* in letters, he succeeded
Claude Fauriel on 25 November 1844. The lat-
ter had held the chair of foreign literature at
the Sorbonne, and Ozanam was his assistant.
Jean-Jacques Ampère described Professor
Ozanam in these words: "He prepared his
lectures like a Benedictine, and delivered them
like an orator." For twelve years he was faithful
to teaching and to his students at the Sorbonne,
which he greatly loved. Nonetheless, he often

was attacked by hostile professors and anar-
chists. He had a lofty concept of the teaching
profession, and sickness alone removed him
from the Sorbonne, where he taught until June
1852. Ozanam was unanimously respected for
his professorial qualities. He was a member of
several foreign academies (Florence, Rome,
Bavaria, etc.), but because of illness, he abandoned the possibility of presenting himself for
membership in the Academy of Inscriptions
and Literature.

Founder

Frédéric earnestly took part in the conference of history promoted by Emmanuel Bailly.
"The subjects are open: history, philosophy,
literature, everything is permitted," he wrote
to a friend. The influence of the forty-year-
old Bailly on the thought and action of the
Christians of his day is remarkable. He had the
idea of these meetings at which students would
be gathered, whether Catholics or not. People
have rightly said that this was an intellectual
apostolate.

Frédéric wanted to have a more concrete
application. He and some friends who assembled on 23 April 1833 decided to answer the
attacks leveled by anticlericals. They would
adopt and adapt the principle of a gathering
of young Catholics who would go to the poor.

They agreed to found a Conference of Charity, a little group set up to visit the poorest of the poor. This grew quite quickly with the help and support of Sister Rosalie Rendu, a Daughter of Charity.

Husband

His love life began late. Should he get married? Should he become a priest? Ozanam reflected on this, knowing that he would have to take some decision about his adult life. With Providence watching over him, Frédéric met Amélie Soulacroix, daughter of the rector of the Academy of Lyons. He fell in love with this young girl, nineteen years old — he was twenty-seven. They married on Wednesday, 23 June 1841, in the church of St. Nizier in Lyons. The young couple spent a long honeymoon in Italy, and then moved to Paris, where Frédéric became an assistant professor at the Sorbonne. They would have twelve years of an admirable love. Amélie gave birth, on 24 July 1845, to Marie. She would be her father's joy, but he would always be concerned for his daughter's health (the memory of the loss of his young brothers and sisters tormented him). Ozanam was an attentive husband for his dear Amélie, the perfect wife. Many gave witness to their simple but admirable life.

In 1853, during a long stay in Italy (the minister had granted him a time for study, as well as rest), his health declined. On his fortieth birthday he wrote his testament, a page admirable for its faith and love for those women and men he loved. Finally, the illness triumphed. Frédéric wanted to return to France. With his brothers, on 31 August 1853 he took ship at Livorno for Marseilles where his in-laws were waiting. He died there on Thursday, 8 September 1853, the feast of the Nativity of Mary. He rests now in the chapel of the Carmelite church in Paris, dressed in the Franciscan habit, like Dante, whom he brought back from oblivion, and like Francis of Assisi, whose fervent disciple he was.

Ozanam's forty years were lived in an extremely troubled period: France had seven changes of government, and experienced two revolutions, in July 1830 and February 1848, along with uprisings in 1830, 1832, 1833, 1848, the *canut* revolts in 1831 and 1834, the cholera epidemics of 1832 and 1849, the assassination attempt against Louis-Philippe in 1835, etc. The industrialization of the country was moving full speed ahead. On 24 August 1997, when he met John Paul II at the airport, Prime Minister Lionel Jospin offered this homage to Frédéric Ozanam: "This man of faith, insight, and passion could not remain unmoved by misery and social injustice."

Abbreviations

Letters

1	*Lettres*, vol. 1 Lecoffre et Cie, 1865.
2	*Lettres*, vol. 2, Lecoffre et Cie, 1865.
AIL	Letter to Henri d'Aillaud Caseneuve.
BEN	Letter to Charles Benoît.
CHA	Letter to Joseph de Champagny.
COL	Letter to Gustave Colas de la Noue.
COZ	Letter to Charles Ozanam.
CUR	Letter to Léonce Curnier.
DUG	Letter to Prosper Dugas.
FAL	Letter to Ernest Falconnet.
FOI	Letter to Théophile Foisset.
FOR	Letter to Hippolyte Fortoul.
FRA	Letter to Salvat Franchisteguy.
HAR	Letter to Benoîte et Louis Haraneder.
HAV	Letter to Ernest Havet.
HOM	Letter to Charles Hommais.
JAN	Letter to Louis Janmot.
JJA	Letter to Jean-Jacques Ampère.

LAL   Letter to François Lallier.

LET   Letter to Auguste Le Taillandier.

MAR   Letter to Abbé Henri Maret.

MAT   Letter to Auguste Materne.

PEN   Letter to Fr. Tommaso Pendola.

PIS   The Prayer at Pisa, 23 April 1853.

TOM   Letter to Nicolo Tomaseo.

VEL   Letter to Ferdinand Velay.

N.B.   Each reference to a letter has the number 1 or 2 to indicate the volume from which the passage was taken

Books

AME   Correspondance d'Amélie et de Frédéric, *L'Anneau d'Or*, 1953.

AMP   Jean-Jacques Ampère, preface to Œuvres complètes de A. F. Ozanam, 1855.

BA   Louis Baunard, *Frédéric Ozanam d'après sa correspondance*, Paris, 1912; English: *Ozanam in His Correspondence*, Dublin, 1925.

BEAT   Cérémonie de béatification de Frédéric Ozanam, 22 August 1997.

BIS   Arthur Biset, "Monsieur Ozanam professeur," *Echos de la littérature étrangère et des Beaux-arts*, 6 (1846).

CEN   *Ozanam. Livre du Centenaire*, Paris, 1913.

CER   Frédéric Ozanam, Discours au Cercle catholique, 1842.

CHO   Charles Ozanam, *Vie de Frédéric Ozanam*, 1861.

CID   Frédéric Ozanam, *Voyage au pays du Cid*, 1853.

CIV   Frédéric Ozanam, *La Civilisation au ve siècle*, 1851.

DCOM   Frédéric Ozanam, Vingt-quatrième leçon droit commercial, 1840.

DEB   Jean-Jacques Ampère, *Journal des débats*, 9, 12 October 1853.

DRO   Frédéric Ozanam, Cours de droit commercial, Lyons, 1839-1840.

EN   *L'Ère nouvelle*, 1848-1849.

FLO   Frédéric Ozanam, Discours à Florence, 30 January 1853.

GAU   Léon Gautier, *Portraits du xixe siècle, historiens et critiques,* vol. 2, Paris, 1894-1895.

GOB   Frédéric Ozanam, Discours à de jeunes ouvriers, 1848.

LAC   Henri-Dominique Lacordaire, *Frédéric Ozanam*, Paris, 1855.

NOA   Amélie Ozanam, Notes biographiques.

POU   Frédéric Poulin, Éloge de Frédéric Ozanam, Tours, 1861.

PER   Henri Perreyve, *M. Frédéric Ozanam*, Lyons, 1853.

QUI   Edgar Quinet, *Histoire de mes idées, 1815 et 1840,* Paris, 1858.

1

Faith in Time of Trials

How many times I have seen my father
and mother weep, since out of fourteen
children, Heaven left them only three!

(CHA2)

*A*t Frédéric Ozanam's birth in 1813, high
infant mortality was a major scourge:
it reached as high as one-third of live births
by the end of the eighteenth century. Even if
mortality was declining, thanks to vaccina-
tion against smallpox from 1796, as well as
progress in the art of childbirth, the death of
children under one year of age was still one out
of six in 1850. In our days, this drama is con-
siderably less frequent, but no matter what the
age or the reason, the death of a child is always
a cruel trial for parents. Hope in the future
life and recourse to prayer can help a family
overcome this tragedy. During the nineteenth
century, especially in upper-class families, an
only child became the norm. He or she became
precious and acquired new value. Then nurses
were rediscovered. Wealthy families confided
their infants to nurses who often lived in the

country, where hygienic conditions were very defective. These women would take on several infants to increase their poor income, but their mother's milk was sometimes unhealthy. In this way, Frédéric's parents lost several children. Frédéric was the fifth out of fourteen children. He benefitted from the attention that his sister Elisa gave him.

> I had a sister, a beloved sister, who, together with my mother, was my teacher. Her lessons were so sweet and well presented and appropriate to my childish understanding that I found genuine pleasure in them.
>
> (MAT1)

He recalled his dear oldest sister in several letters and in the preface of his book, *History of Civilization in the Fifth Century*:

> My sister, my first teacher, intelligent, and pious as the angels that she has gone to join.
>
> (CIV)

When Elisa died at nineteen, little Frédéric was plunged into the deepest grief.

> I was seven when my sister, my good sister, died. I certainly shared the common sorrow. Oh, the grief I had!
>
> (MAT1)

His childhood was thus stamped with the death of eleven brothers and sisters. It was likewise stamped, and profoundly so, with the

family's piety. He could follow the examples
of his father, his mother, and his sister, whose
faith let him overcome the mourning as it came
along. Although we know little of his father's
religious practice, Frédéric recalled in a letter
of 15 January 1831, how he was instructed.

> This Catholicism so dear to my child-
> hood was taught me at that time by the
> mouth of an excellent mother, and it
> has often nourished my spirit and my
> heart through its lovely recollections
> and its even more beautiful hopes.
>
> (FOR1)

She lived out her faith with conviction
through her attendance at Mass, the recitation
of the rosary, the celebration of the feasts of
the family's patron saints, as well as through
her active membership over many years in an
association of working women, the *Veilleuses*
(the Night-Watchers), organized to go one-by-
one to watch over the sick poor. She believed
firmly in the communion of saints, as Frédéric
Ozanam recalled:

> I saw many people envious of my moth-
> er's happiness in having three children
> who remained faithful to the Catholic
> Faith, and in having in heaven eleven
> other children praying for her.
>
> (LAL2)

> When I had the happiness of receiving
> Communion, when the Savior came

> to visit me, it seemed to me that she followed him into my pitiful heart, just as she followed him on so many occasions when he was brought as Viaticum into poor houses. That is why I believe firmly in the real presence of my mother around me.
>
> (FAL2)

She inculcated the same religious practices in Frédéric: attendance at Mass, preparation for confessions and for his first communion. They prayed as a family, a practice that has very often disappeared in our times. Might this explain the lukewarmness of many young people? He often thanked God for having given him such a mother.

> It pleased you to have formed this holy woman; at her knees I learned a fear of you, and in her glance your love.
>
> (PIS)

We too should bless the Lord for the grace he granted to Frédéric. Let us thank him likewise for all the mothers who have traced out the right road for their children through their faith, their courage, and their self-denial.

After a stay of several years in Italy, the family returned to Lyons in November 1816, to live in an apartment at 5, rue de Pizay, near the Fine-Arts Museum. They stayed there until the death of the father in 1837. The building is quite fine, with exposed stonework around an interior courtyard. Frédéric grew up in an exceptional family environment. His father was a physician at the Hotel-Dieu hospital of Lyons, and also had his own patients. At his father's death, Frédéric believed that a third of his visits were given for free to the needy. He would be recognized as the "physician of the poor" for having lived out a concrete faith in their service. The family lived in relative but sufficient ease.

> I want to thank God for having me born in one of these positions, at the boundary between need and comfort, which accustom us to privations but without leaving us absolutely bereft of any enjoyment. In such a situation, we could not fall asleep having satisfied all our desires, but we were not distracted either by constant concern for what we needed.
>
> (LAL1)

In this atmosphere, Frédéric's faith grew. Beyond his regular attendance at Mass, he read the Bible and frequently made notes in it. Later, with his wife Amélie, he prayed morning and evening. As she wrote: *"His piety was living and consoling. He found in the practice of our holy religion, in the sacraments, the strength of constantly renewed fervor, and in the last days of his life, he found calm, a peace that came from Heaven."* (NOA) He put his faith into practice during his entire life through his visits to the poor, being alert to the Christian questions of his friends as well as to their doubts, in educating little Marie, and in never hesitating to proclaim his faith before his students and colleagues at the Sorbonne.

> If you are nourished by these admirable teachers of the Middle Ages, and of these Fathers [of the Church], they would offer a reading worthy of your noble intelligence. You would not date liberty, tolerance, fraternity, or any of those great political dogmas used by the Revolution as stemming from the Revolution, but rather as descending from Calvary.
>
> (HAV2)

He invites us to do the same, just as he did, with delicacy and humility, without fear of affirming the value of what we live. With Frédéric's help, we should meditate on and defend our faith if needed, and whenever needed. Some will be grateful to us for that. And they will see us as disciples of the Lord.

Reflection Questions

- ☙ What is the quality of my faith: high? Low? Mediocre? What could I do today to nourish my faith and make it grow?

- ☙ Can others perceive my faith through my words and actions? What opportunities lay ahead of me to share my faith with others?

2

His High School Years, and the Influence of Abbé Noirot

Later, the sounds of an unbelieving world reached me. I experienced all the horror of those doubts which gnaw at the heart during the day, and which one finds at night in a bed wet with tears. The lack of certitude about my eternal destiny left me no rest. It was then that a priest philosopher saved me. He put order and light into my thoughts. From then on, I believed with a certain faith and, touched by such a rare gift, I promised God to devote my days to the service of the truth that was giving me peace.

(CIV)

*U*p to age nine and a half, like many children of middle-class families, Frédéric Ozanam was educated only at home by his mother, father, his sister Elisa and his brother Alphonse. Elisa, his older sister, was beautiful and quite intelligent. She had learned music, drawing, and English from her father. Alphonse, awarded a diploma as a doctor of medicine, left, with little enthusiasm on his

43

father's part, for the Seminary of St. Sulpice in October 1822. At the same time, Frédéric was beginning his first year at the royal secondary school of Lyons (today, the Lycée Ampère). Like many such schools at that time, this one was a very unpleasant place. It was located between the Saône and the Rhône Rivers on rue de la Bource, barely 500 meters from his family's apartment. Edgar Quinet, who had been a boarder from 1817 to 1820, gives a less than attractive picture: *"Black buildings, shadowy vaults, locked doors and grilles, damp chapels, and high walls that kept out the sun."* (QUI) One could add the words: collapsing, unhealthy, uncomfortable.

Frédéric made his first communion on Thursday, 11 May 1826, when he finished his third year. He was just thirteen years old. He received the sacrament of confirmation shortly after, and in this way he committed himself to affirm his faith before all. He never backed down from his promise, despite his period of doubt, whether in his family, in the Society of St. Vincent de Paul, in his years as a university professor, or in his years of physical suffering. He was an exceptionally fine boy. Thanks to lessons from his father, he quickly spoke Italian, and when he began school, he learned Latin, as his father had. The study of Greek, Hebrew, and later Sanskrit would follow. During his studies, he learned English and Spanish. After he completed this school in 1830, he studied German, and even spent some time taking a course in drawing. As Lacordaire wrote: *"There was no muse that did not dwell in him."* (LAC)

Frédéric very quickly became one of the top students in his class, and he would graduate at the top of his class. In a long letter to one of the closest friends, Auguste Materne, dated 5 June 1830, he described his school life and his problems as an adolescent. He experienced the troubles of puberty, which he described perfectly:

> Criminal, even licentious, thoughts overwhelmed me, despite myself. I wanted to get rid of them; but I worked too hard at it. My respectable confessor told me not to be worried about them.
>
> (MAT1)

The world may have changed, but young people experience the same issues. Will they find an attentive listener, someone who is discreet and reassuring to those who want to confide in them?

In 1830, France experienced more troubles. The revolution of that year and those that followed, were marked by terrible antireligious events. In Paris, the sack of St. German l'Auxerrois and of the archbishop's residence struck a chord in the people. Passions were unleashed, and they took it out on the clergy. The archbishop himself fled the capital for some time, and sordid stories were published and anticlerical plays performed. Musset exclaimed in his *Confessions d'un enfant du siè- cle:* "The host, this eternal symbol of heavenly love, was used to seal letters." This, of course, rubbed off on the young, many of whom failed to continue to practice their faith after making their first communion. Frédéric had doubts, but he persevered in his religious duties. He prayed, he attended the parish church with his parents, he went to confession regularly, even if this caused him some distress. He wanted to be convinced. He passed through a very diffi- cult period that he later thanked heaven about: *in the age of skepticism, God did me the favor of being born in the faith.* (CIV) Frédéric knew the horrors of doubt, and he no longer knew where he was.

> When I tried to understand talking about unbelievers and unbelief, I started to wonder why I was a believer.
> (CIV)

He expressed this next thought in the intro- duction to his *Civilization in the Fifth Century,* published in 1851.

Holding on tightly to sacred teachings,
I believed I heard them breaking under
my hand.

(CIV)

His professor, Abbé Noirot, was a true spiritual director.

He put order and light into my thoughts.
From then on, I believed with a certain
faith and, touched by such a rare gift,
I promised God to devote my days to
the service of the truth that was giving
me peace.

(CIV)

Abbé Noirot benefitted from an uncommon authority. He became rector of the University of Lyons in 1854 and would be esteemed by all the university authorities, among others the minister of public instruction, Victor Cousin. He would say of Noirot: "Abbé Noirot is the leading professor of philosophy in France. The others send me their books; he sends me men." In addition to his qualities as a professor, Abbé Noirot knew how to lead, how to guide the young man to recover at the very moment that he had to face huge difficulties in living out his faith. His adolescent faith was changing into an adult faith, committed to the service of his family, his students, the Society of St. Vincent de Paul, and of the poor that he would visit. Although some of his friends would definitively turn away from the faith and religious practice, Frédéric would never again be attacked by doubts. He expressed this tranquil faith one last time when he was on his deathbed, in September 1853. He answered a question from his confessor about God and exclaimed:

Why should I fear him? I love him so much!

Just like Frédéric, we are often attacked by doubt, by our lack of faith, by our refusal to allow ourselves to be invaded and helped by the Lord.

> I had doubts and yet I wanted to believe. I pushed doubt away. Though my faith was not solid, I still prefer to believe without reason than to doubt, because that tormented me so.
>
> (MAT1)

In our days, prayer remains one of the specific acts of the Society of St. Vincent de Paul. Every meeting starts and ends with a prayer or a meditation on a text from the Bible or from different writers. In this way, we are only following tradition, the demands of the first Vincentians.

Reflection Questions

ℛ In reviewing the development of my own faith, who were those who most influenced me? How did they influence me, and what were their words or actions that were the most important for me?

❧ Who are those whom I should be helping in their own faith? What words or actions should I be using to be of help and support to them?

3

The Love of Amélie and Frédéric

> So, it is with a sincere brotherly sim-
> plicity that I am announcing my hap-
> piness. It is very great, surpassing all
> my hopes and dreams, and, since last
> Wednesday, the day on which God's
> blessing came down upon my head, I
> am living in a calm, serene, and deli-
> cious enchantment that nothing could
> have prepared me for.
>
> (AMP1)

*F*rédéric was happy on that 23 June 1841, the day of his wedding to Amélie Soulacroix, the daughter of the rector of the University of Lyons. He fully lived out this moment, and experienced, I am sure, the same emotions that every baptized person does on this occasion. But we cannot, of course, find the words to speak or write it, to have others experience and share this sensation of complete fullness, the fruit of this divine sacrament. The mutual promise made by two persons, for their entire life, is no small matter and deserves some time of reflection before making this definitive decision. In our age — but was this untrue even previously? — do people not understand that this engagement "for better, for worse" is a contract? This is such a serious matter that the contract is entered into in the presence of civil authorities, and for us Christians, in the presence of a priest who testifies that these two persons are joining together for life. Frédéric often questioned himself before taking the step of marriage. He hesitated long between joining a religious order (certainly with the Dominicans of his good friend Lacordaire), or getting married. He clearly understood that he would have to make a decision about how to lead his adult life. At age twenty-two, he wondered:

> It seems to me that for some time now I have been experiencing the precursor symptoms of a new level of emotions, and this frightens me. I sense within myself a great emptiness that neither friendship nor study will fill. Is this God? Is this a creature? If it is a creature, I pray that it will take some time in coming, when I have become worthy. I pray that it will bring with it the necessary external charms so as not to leave any room for regret. But I especially pray that this creature, she, will come with an excellent soul, will bring great virtue, and will be much better than I am.

> (CUR1)

He was afraid of marriage, as he wrote to Lallier in 1837:

It is especially this perpetuity of commitment that is full of terror for me, and that is why I cannot keep from weeping whenever I attend a wedding.

(LAL1)

Often, he was even sarcastic when he thought about this sacrament.

The Holy Virgin and my mother and many other women will make me forgive many things in these daughters of Eve. But I declare that, in general, I do not understand them. Their sensitivity is sometimes wonderful, but their intelligence is shallow and desperately inconsequential... and then to get married in such a society, no holds barred, to a human, mortal, weak, miserable creature, no matter how perfect she is?

(LAL1)

This was a widely-shared opinion among men in the middle of the nineteenth century. But even in today's world, are we sure that we have uprooted this attitude?

Providence was watching over him and placed on his path a young woman from Lyons like he was, nineteen years old, who was giving loving care to her younger brother who was gravely ill. Amélie's qualities quickly won over Frédéric: gentleness, foresight, love of others, and generosity. He fell deeply in love with this girl who radiated throughout the household. When he returned to Paris in December 1840, he wrote:

May God guard the woman whom
he seems to have chosen for me, and
whose smile is the first ray of sunshine
that I have had in my life since the
death of my dear father. You will find
me tenderly overwhelmed! But I am
not hiding from it, and I cannot sometimes keep from laughing over it, me,
who used to think that I had a heart of
bronze.

(LAL1)

Frédéric had difficulty realizing what was
happening to him. His life had greatly changed.
He was far away from Amélie during the whole
time of their engagement and he suffered for it,
since he was teaching at the Sorbonne, while
she was living in Lyons. This is similar to couples today whom the demands of work often
keep apart, even for a long time. Amélie asked
him: "share everything with me, so that I can
say We." He answered: *"From now on, we will
say We."* (AME) Here, too, there was a certain
apprenticeship in living as a couple. It was no
easier in his time than in ours. Certain letters
show that he had a hard time getting used to
this, but the strength of couples with faith in
each other lets them smooth out the difficulties. Sometimes there was tension between
them; it would be surprising if there was not,
but under God's protection, with the support
of prayer and recourse to the sacraments, the
difficulties were smoothed over.

You will pardon me a lot, because I
have loved too much; as for me, I will
become worthy of your indulgence by
purifying my love

(AME).

These letters show that those days were a
happy time, and, instead of as onlookers, they
allow us to witness the joys, the sorrows, and
the cares of this couple. What will we leave to
the following generations, we who use smart
phones and e-mails but do not let our pens
wander to tell stories, to tell our stories, to
question, and to question ourselves? Curiously,
in our days, children ask their parents to write
down their past for them, perhaps because they
understand that these stories risk being lost
forever.

These twelve years of marriage were a
dozen years of perfect and deep happiness.
The birth of Marie in July 1845 would be a
blessing for Amélie and Frédéric. I think that
all parents understand this. And what joy, then,
to announce the happy birth! We could even
tell a passerby. The happy time of marriage
would be interrupted by death. But what faith
for Amélie and for Frédéric during the long
passage toward 8 September 1853, the date of
his leaving for the Father. Frédéric penned a
poetic description of marriage for us:

> There are two glasses: in one, there is purity, modesty, innocence; in the other there is complete love, devotion, and the deathless consecration of a man to a person who is weaker than he is; he did not know her yesterday, but with her today he is happy to spend the rest of his life. These two glasses both have to be full for their union to be mutual and for heaven to bless it.
>
> (CIV)

All his life, Frédéric showed us how the couple was a mutual enrichment and, how, with Amélie, he provided the example of a complete faithfulness in marriage. Both of them showed us how to live a total love in all the senses perceived by the ancient Greeks: *philía,* éros, *agapé.*

> When God brings two souls together, he grants happiness as their reward. He never leaves them out of these conditions. It is here that we experience in its depths the mystery of conjugal union.
>
> (AME)

Reflection Questions

- ❧ How has deep personal love touched my life, whether married or single? What can I do now or in the coming days to nourish my love? What actions, great or small, can I perform to help in this?

ఔ Whom can I help in their own lives when love is weak or absent? What specific gestures of support could I offer?

4
I'm a Father!

So many graces stabilized my vocation
in this world and put an end to keeping
my family apart. A new grace arrived
to make me know probably the greatest
joy that one can experience here below:
I'm a father.

(FOI2)

We should specify briefly the graces
that Frédéric mentioned at the beginning of this letter: he had recently learned of
his appointment as professor of the chair of
foreign literature at the Sorbonne, and the
family came together, since his in-laws, the
Soulacroix, left Lyons to move to Paris. It was
a heartfelt cry that Frédéric sent to his friend
Foisset on 7 August 1845, when he announced
the birth of Marie, his first child, born on 24
July. This letter makes us feel the enormous
bliss of a delighted new father. The birth of the
first child of a couple is a unique moment, and
Frédéric describes it in enthusiastic detail.

Oh, what a moment when, kneeling at
Amélie's bed, I saw her final push, and,

at the same time, my child came into
this world.

(HAR2)

Oh, Monsieur, what a moment when
I heard my child's first cry! Or when I
saw this little creature, this immortal
creature whom God had placed into
our hands, who brought me so much
happiness and so many obligations.

(FOI2)

A couple's other births could never have the
same intensity, even if they are just as hoped
and wished for, and just as anticipated. This
birth had been hoped for since their marriage,
but the Ozanams were becoming desperate.
Amélie suffered two miscarriages. Far from
Paris, she rested and regained her strength. On
6 August 1842, Frédéric listed the visits that he
had made to families in trouble, one of which
had children to whom Amélie offered a little
gift:

... so that these tiny creatures will pray
for you, and for both of us, to keep far
from us the sorrow of this year, and to
obtain for us the little angel that our
home is waiting for.

(AME)

The months passed with new dashed hopes,
but there was one new attempt that Frédéric
mentioned when he wrote to Amélie: *"for this
dear hope that delighted us last spring and that we*

would like to see flower again." (AME) For a young couple to wait month after month after more than four years together was difficult. They loved each other and ardently hoped for a large family (an unfulfilled wish, since only Marie arrived to delight their household). Frédéric spoke in this way about their married harmony:

> There is this impossibility of being separated from one another, this unbearable wrenching that is being apart.
>
> (AME)

Each of the proposals that Frédéric used expressed the love he had for the future mother of their child. It is very difficult to separate married love from parental love. The period of pregnancy, which men experience so differently from women, is the occasion for a new deepening of their love. The Ozanams were very close, despite the occasional little quarrels and misunderstandings: *Here I am, begging you to forgive my faults and the distress they have caused you,* (AME) — an expression that lets us come closer in our way of understanding our married life and our parental life, with its joys and cares, its little delights and weaknesses. With Frédéric we appreciate knowing a Blessed who experienced the same difficulties that many couples have: such as being apart from one's wife, the mother of one's children; or those "delicate" times at the end of each month. This is the reason why, among many others, he is so close to us, Christians of the twenty-first century. It may not be thoroughly modern to look to lay saints, married and parents, for examples. Listen to him describe for us his life as a marriage partner, his life as a dad, and follow him. Frédéric took care of the future mother in a very concrete way:

> Ask his [Doctor Richard's] advice about how to handle things in case of a pregnancy; the headaches that you had last winter.
>
> (AME)

For a Christian couple, the husband and wife cannot be separated. Amélie was the wife who completed Frédéric. Each enriched the other.

> You will be the ray of light ever present in my thoughts.
>
> (AME)

What husband has never experienced this feeling? Frédéric grew weary waiting for the joy of the birth of a child, even *if we have to put off to happier times the joy of seeing these little angels, who owe their lives to us, playing around us.*

> (AME)

After Marie's birth, the proud father wrote tenderly:

> There is a pretty crib in the bedroom, and under the blue curtain there is a little angel that, two weeks ago, the good Lord and the Blessed Virgin sent us.
>
> (AME)

Later, when he was in Douai to take his baccalaureate examination, he was worried about "little Marie's" health, whom he would sometimes affectionately call Nini, and about Amélie.

> Try to get well and put on a little weight, and bring to a fitting conclusion little Marie's convalescence.
>
> (AME)

In some of his letters, Frédéric delighted in speaking about their child; in them we uncover his careful attention to his daughter.

> Yesterday, I had a dinner with a little girl who wasn't causing any bother at all.
>
> (AME)

> Since the Blessed Virgin loves good children, I have often prayed for Marie. Also, I am very sure that Marie will be perfectly obedient and will never fuss.
>
> (AME)

While on a trip to London, he sent her this message on the feast of the Assumption, 15 August:

I want to wish you a happy feast day.
It is a very big feast day, since it is a
feast of the Blessed Virgin. She is called
Marie just like you, and because she
gave her name to you, you should give
her your heart. Ask her to pray for you
so that you will be good and the good
Lord will love you.

(AME)

We will begin her education early, at
the same time that [our little angel] will
start ours. I realize now that heaven
sent her to us to teach us many things
and to make us better.

(FOI2)

A few days afterwards, Frédéric wrote to his
daughter's godfather:

I know of nothing sweeter on earth
than when I come home to find my
beloved wife and my dear child in her
arms. I then become the third member
of the group.

(LAL2)

This same touching and peaceful scene
takes place daily, in all parts of the world, for
all couples who love each other.

Reflection Questions

ℭ What have I learned from my own children, or those of others, that has brought
me closer to God? How have their lives

affected mine, especially for the better?
What is my response in prayer?

ର How do I deal with the inevitable tensions that physical separation brings?
Am I able to stand on my own? Do
I have a life of my own apart from a
spouse or loved one?

5

Friends

Your nice letter consoled me greatly.
Really, nothing is more consoling than
remembering those to whom one is
closely attached in the heart. I think
you already said it: the enjoyments of
a family are very precious, blood has
its innate and unavoidable rights; but
friendship has acquired and sacred
rights, enjoyments which never give
out. Relatives and friends are the two
sorts of companions that God has given
us along the road of life. The presence
of the one cannot make us forget the
absence of the others.

(LAL1)

For Frédéric, friendship was a precious gift.
Amélie would say: "He made a profession
of affections," and Frédéric confirmed this.

I have never been able to overlook my
friends, but their memory for me is
infinitely more precious because revolutions separate so many who used to
be beloved.

(DUG2)

From his secondary school days, he made friends with a group of students. He would do the same in Paris during his studies, and he would carry on a strict and regular correspondence with them. In it, friendship would be the leading word for the happy moments, such as the marriage of his friends: *"As you have shared my sorrow amid your happy plans, I, too, surrounded by sadness, smiled at your coming happiness."* (LET1) He once had a pleasant hike: *"We talk a lot and in different ways; we take some punch and cook and return completely happy in groups of four or five."* (FAL1) He announced the creation of the first Conference of the Society outside Paris: *"Your letter filled me with joy. I have not kept this joy to myself, since I told it to some of my friends who belong to our little group."* (CUR1) There were also unhappy stairs to climb, and on many happy occasions, Frédéric would write tender and peaceful words to friends who had lost a loved one. He always mentioned his faith and the union between the living and the dead. When he was twenty-five, he supposed that he had already passed a third of his life expectancy. This would be quickly verified.

> Your unhappy news moved me to tears. Let me congratulate you for the faith that is supporting you in such a great trial.
>
> (LAL2)

A friend is a part of ourselves, someone who gives us help and advice, someone we can share our reactions with on the great questions of life, on our faith. It is indispensable to have true friends; they listen without speaking, they accept our silence, and they encourage us. Frédéric gave himself to this to help one friend during his university studies, to counsel another in his future plans and reawaken him in his faith.

> I realized that you are somewhat reticent with me on just one point, since you doubtless fear to open your soul to me: I mean, to speak about faith! I am certain that in this matter, revolutions have occurred in your spirit that you never told me about, and in which, nevertheless, I would love to take part, not, of course, to teach you — I couldn't do that, but to share your worries a little and to offer you some consolation.
>
> (FAL1)

What a beautiful letter this was, written in 1834 to Falconnet, in which we understand the attention that Frédéric offers to his friends in trouble! He does not hold back from reproaching him for not have spoken to him, for failing to confide in him, since he might have helped him and alleviated his doubts. His faith is not just personal and inward, but a faith that communicates, a faith that he wants to spread among his friends. He had no hesitation to say what he was thinking, or to mention Him in whom he believed. He laid out his convictions with a frankness and simplicity that we never (ever?) dare to proclaim and even less hand on to others, even when we are in a small group or in a meeting of the Conference. Why are we afraid of offering our Christian witness? It is strange to realize that we (that I) do not dare to mention our faith, although that is what many expect from us. We are afraid to give witness, even when others want us to confidently proclaim our faith in the thrice-holy God. Many of those who seek do not find Christians proud of what they live and ready to help and encourage them. Thus it is that:

> We Catholics are punished for having placed more trust in the genius of our great men than in the power of our God....

> We are punished for relying on these thinking reeds, no matter how melodious they are; they are broken under our hands. We have to look for help on high. We do not heed a weak stick to travel the earth; there are, instead, two wings that carry the angels: faith and charity.

> (CUR1)

Frédéric, for his part, did not hesitate to ask for moral and spiritual help from a friend:

> I feel better when I have poured out
> my heart into the heart of a friend who
> is a better person than I am. Without
> realizing it, in this way you are doing
> me some good; and these lines that
> you will read in a few days will have
> strengthened my heart and will ener-
> gize me for some time.
>
> (CUR1)

We often sin through fear of what someone might say, through human respect. What a shame not to risk telling a true friend of our discouragements, our fears, but also our faith in man and especially in God! Frédéric also experienced some falling out with a few of his friends who distanced themselves from him or left the group, or who, like Lamennais, whom he was very close to, broke with the Church and abandoned the faith. But even in these circumstances, he had some saving words to bring hope, words which were waiting for reconciliation and peace in the future.

> Let us find ourselves at least in the
> presence of God, because we cannot
> find ourselves united in the presence of
> men; since we cannot talk together, let
> us pray for each other, and this will be
> even better.
>
> (HOM1)

How hard it is for us to adopt such a generous Christian attitude, trying to reconcile instead of breaking down the differences, of asking the help of the Lord or of the Blessed Virgin, in whom Frédéric had such absolute confidence!

Reflection Questions

- ⊂ When was the last time I thanked God in prayer for friends and family? What can I do, besides prayer, to show concretely how much I appreciate them?

- ⊂ Do I really have a friend with whom I can share my deepest thoughts, my hopes and struggles? How can I develop such a relationship if I do not currently have one?

6

The Development of the Society of St. Vincent de Paul

By starting small we can do great things, like Jesus Christ, who, from his tiny crib was raised to the glory of Tabor.

(FLO)

*T*his short sentence is taken from a talk that Frédéric gave in 1853 to the members of the Society of St. Vincent de Paul in Florence. He reviewed the first years of Society's foundation, its development and expansion through the world. After the painful period that he had while a teenager, Frédéric overcame his doubts. After he was strengthened, he experienced the wish to participate in the development of the faith. With a convert's zeal, he wanted to share his happiness.

That is why, by the strength of reason my soul found again precisely this Catholicism taught me by the mouth of an excellent mother.

(FLO)

He said the following to his friends whom he invited them to join him:

> But don't you experience like me the desire, the need to have outside this militant Conference, another meeting, composed exclusively of Christian friends, completely devoted to charity? Doesn't it seem to you that now is the time to join action to words, and to affirm by works the vitality of our faith?
>
> (FOR1)

Severe discussions arose in Paris between Christian students and those who demanded that they make their faith believable.

> You are right to speak about the past. Christianity did marvels in the past; but today, Christianity is dead. Indeed, what are you doing, you who boast of being Catholics? Where are the works that show your faith and which can move us to accept and respect it?
>
> (FLO)

Their proposals started them moving. In answer, some friends joined Frédéric.

> May our acts agree with our faith. What should we do? What should we be doing to be truly Catholic, other than what pleases God the most? Let us, then, care for the neighbor, as Jesus did, and place our faith under the aegis of charity.
>
> (FLO)

He let his plans mature. His first reflections turned toward a concrete orientation: faith and its application in action, and in action toward the poor. Did not the Lord tell us: "Why do you call me, 'Lord, Lord,' but not do what I command?" (Lk 6:46). Frédéric and a small group then began a Conference of charity to come to the aid of the weakest. "Conference of charity" as a title came from the name "Conference of history," where many students gathered under the direction of Emmanuel Bailly, who had founded study groups. They had many discussions and remade the world (a large number of them were law students). On this basis they adopted a name emphasizing charity. The rapid development of this first group showed that the Lord was with them, and that he is still with us. Prayer had its place in that first meeting, and it is still observed in every meeting. It is a prayer of praise for favors obtained, of petition for the families that we accompany in their need, of adoration of God who guides us and whom we see in our midst, as he has promised: "For where two or three are gathered together in my name, there am I in the midst of them" (Mt 18:20).

At the beginning of the nineteenth century, when the media — except for newspapers and posters — did not exist, and where public transport was limited to coaches, the speedy development of the Society of St. Vincent de

Paul is remarkable, and it shows a supernatural assistance. Those young men engaging in direct action showed the way for others to follow. Their happiness was great when another conference began, this time in Nimes, in October 1834.

> God and the poor will bless you, and we, whom you will surpass, will be proud and happy to count you as our brothers. The promise we made is carried out in this way: you are the first echo to answer our weak voice. Perhaps others will soon follow; and then the greater merit of our Parisian society will be to have begun to form others like us. You only need one thread to begin a cloth.
>
> (CUR1)

He repeatedly shared this happiness. Despite numerous difficulties, he would always be an optimist about the future of his "dear little society," and he would be an active promoter of the development of Conferences in France and in Europe. He would rejoice in the founding of groups in distant lands, such as Palestine, the United States, or Mexico, who began their activities during his lifetime. When he could, he made it his duty to create Conferences and visit them.

> In Bayonne, I find a very flourishing Conference of St. Vincent de Paul. It is

filled with our original spirit, and tire-
less in good works.

(LAL2)

He traveled widely. In London, during the
Universal Exposition of 1851 with a confrere
from London he visited, *some of those poor folks,
and I realized that the English would need great
virtue and courage to personally help these horrible
miseries. Our confreres do marvelous good, and I am
delighted to have spent an evening with them.*

(COZ2)

It would be same in Spain, Belgium, and
Germany, and, of course, in Italy where he
stayed on many occasions. Toward the end of
his life, he would still begin several Italian conferences, especially in Tuscany.

Modern Italy no longer builds cathedrals; but at least there are Conferences
of St. Vincent de Paul that are growing.
I had the consolation of spending several hours with our confreres in Genoa.

(FRA)

Amid our present difficulties, we continue
our duty. This has developed in many ways to
respond to the new types of poverty in our days:
loneliness of all sorts, housing, work, broken
families, etc. But we still maintain our basic
goals: family visits wherever the person lives:
in the home, on the street, among the homeless,
or in hospitals, prisons, or retirement homes,

plus prayer, our indispensable nourishment. We have to move forward. We should not suppose that it was better in the past. Frédéric in his time used to complain in the columns of Ère *nouvelle* about the lack of purpose and the timidity of good people. He founded this newspaper after the 1848 revolution with Frs. Lacordaire and Maret.

> Let us keep our head and place our confidence in Providence, assured that God has made our work his own and wishes to spread it throughout the world and fill it with his blessings.
>
> (FLO)

Examples abound of the effective presence of the Lord in each of the thousand conferences of France, and the 45,000 others in the 145 countries where the Society is at work.

Reflection Questions

- ☙ Is my faith limited to my private life of prayer and meditation? Apart from works of financial generosity, what do I do, or what can I start doing, to be of service to those most in need of love, friendship or other kinds of help?

- ☙ If age or health or handicaps keep me from an active outreach in charity, how can I still be of service? What specific acts of kindness and support can I do now? Is my natural timidity holding me back?

7

An Apostolate in Service
of the Poor

If we do not know how to love God
as the saints loved him, that is certainly because we do not see God
only through the eyes of faith, and our
faith is so weak! But we see men, the
poor, with the eyes of flesh. They are
there, and we can put our finger and
our hand on their wounds and on the
marks of the crown of thorns visible
on their forehead. Lack of faith has
no place here. We should fall down at
their feet and say with the apostle: You
are our masters, and we will be your
servants. You are the visible images
of this God whom we do not see, but
whom we believe we love in loving you.

(JAN1)

*W*hen he was very young, Frédéric had
the burning wish to have Christianity
reclaim its first place. He would always be an
activist in his soul. When he was just eighteen,
in January 1831, he wrote to two friends:

I will be delighted if some friends gather
around me! Then, if we join our efforts,
we could create something together,
and others would join us, and perhaps

one day all society will join under this protective shade: Catholicism, full of youth and strength, will rise up suddenly upon the world.

(FOR1)

His primary ambition was to begin, through his intellectual gifts, a campaign for a rebirth of Christianity, to show "religion glorified by history," according to this expression of Jean-Jacques Ampère: *"Perpetuity, the Catholicism of religious ideas, truth, excellence, the beauty of Christianity."* (AMP) He was not yet dreaming of starting a charitable work. The preparations for his literary and historical work would serve him well when, beginning in 1832, he was engaged in an intellectual apostolate in the Sorbonne, where his friends and he offered replies to the rationalist ideas of certain professors.

What is most useful in this work is to show to the young students that one can be Catholic and still have common sense; that one can love both religion and liberty. Finally, it is to draw them out of religious indifference and accustom them to grave and serious discussions.

(FAL1)

In a letter to Ernest Falconnet, written in March 1833, Frédéric presented his view on the action to take:

There are about ten of us, even more closely united with bonds of spirit and

heart, devoted friends with no secrets,
who open their souls to talk in turn
about their joys, their hopes, and their
sorrows.

(FAL1)

Shortly after, they met to found the first
Conference of charity. It was agreed
from the first day that they would visit
the poor in their homes, and that they
would ask the Daughters of Charity to
show them the most needy families.
Prayer opened and closed the meeting,
and they took up a collection each time.
Each of the members soon had a family to whom they brought vouchers [for
bread and meat] purchased from Sister
Rosalie, since the Conference was not
wealthy enough to have any in its own
name.

(FLO)

One hundred seventy-eight years later, the
members of the Conferences, from all over the
world, still apply the same principles:

- visiting the families recommended
  to us by social services, the parishes,
  the neighbors, or those whom the
  Conference has already helped;

- spiritual exercises either within the
  Conference by a moment of prayer,
  often accompanied by a spiritual advi-
  sor (a priest, a religious, a lay person) or
  outside such as having Masses for the

intention of the families that have been visited and for our confreres, plus days of recollection and retreat.

The primary mission of Vincentians is accompaniment in friendship through a regular visit, or by the welcome given in places opened for this through the responsibility of the members, all volunteers, of the Conference (or of the regional council). This is one of our characteristics: an association of volunteers who are helped, when needed, by "indispensable salaried persons," since it is genuinely essential at the national level and in the Welcome Centers. But all our 134 listed actions accomplished throughout the year are done by men and women who give of their time and their energy to support and relieve the neediest.

We insist on a group of volunteers who are truly committed for the long term, instead of just for some small service given when chance allows. Our activity happens every day of the year and not only at key moments, such as Christmas, even if the poor need a warm presence during that time when loneliness and deprivation are the most painful. But we, too, need support, especially for new committed and competent members, since the job is difficult and delicate, and it comes after our professional or familial occupations are finished. When we go to see a sick person who is tired and lonely, that is when we understand God's plan. Even when he was desperately ill, Frédéric still visited families in the Mouffetard neighborhood of Paris.

> How many times, burdened by some interior suffering and worried about my continuing ill health, have I walked, full of my own sadness, into the dwelling of a poor person confided to my care. There, because so many unfortunates have more to complain about than I, I scolded myself for being discouraged. I felt strengthened even more against sorrow, and I thanked that poor person who had consoled and strengthened me through the sight of his own sufferings. From that time on, how could I not love him?
>
> (FAL1)

For Frédéric, to avoid discouragement it was essential to count on the support of the group and on the Lord. He had the habit of saying: *"Beware of discouragement; it is the death of the soul."* (LAL1) He asks us to place our confidence in the hands of the Lord, to follow his will, and to realize that it is he, the divine artisan.

> Although we may be useless servants, we are not allowed to become lazy ones.
>
> (LAL1)

I often pray over — and I am not the only Vincentian to do this — the parable of the Good Samaritan. He was a man attacked by robbers,

left for dead by the side of the road, helped by
a traveler. Jesus is not afraid of using a stranger
to help a wounded man. And what kind of
stranger is he? A Samaritan. A member of a
sect despised by Jews. We could easily trans-
fer this to our own time. Frédéric "translated"
this story by asking men to relieve the misery
of so many kinds of persons wounded in life
(by pouring oil on their wounds), and likewise
to struggle against this misery by becoming
involved in activities to make it disappear.

> May charity do what justice alone
> would be unable to accomplish.
>
> (LAL1)

From the beginning, we have affirmed our
attachment to the word charity, although others may replace it with "solidarity." The term
"charity" as used here does not simply denote
assistance, but has the force of love for others
(our neighbor). The Society of St. Vincent de
Paul proclaims and insists: "Charity is ever
young."

Reflection Questions

℞ Read over the parable of the Good
Samaritan (Lk 10:29-37) and pray about
it. How does this central story resonate
with you today? What concrete action
of loving charity is called for?

ᘓ Think about the difference between assistance and charity. Do my acts of charitable giving involve me in any way in the real lives of others? Do I even know the name of one poor person?

8

The Problem of Collaboration

It is impossible to be blind: the Society
has run into challenges everywhere.
Although in Lyons it has not incurred
the blame of Church authorities, and
though some venerable priests have
encouraged the Society, it has not
ceased being the object of humiliations
from many laypersons: the swelled
heads of orthodoxy, Council fathers all
lined up in rows, but in stylish trousers
with straps under foot. You cannot
imagine the intrigues, the pettiness,
the arguments, the nit-picking, the
assaults that those people, with the best
faith in the world, have used against us.
The most esteemed have been brought
along by the crowd, and we have had to
suffer greatly from them, even if they
once loved us.

(LAL1)

*T*his text shows the different sorts of
attacks that the Society of St. Vincent de
Paul had to face from the time of its foundation in 1833. Internal differences sometimes
nearly caused it to break up, but Frédéric's vig-
ilant wisdom always restored unity. The first

Conference of charity had experienced some time of disruption. The ambience was so warm that it seemed difficult to enlarge the group to admit new members. Time was needed to accept this. Even today it is often the same. How many times have we not heard this reflection during meetings: "We are large enough; let's wait before doing any more"? The more a Conference can count on its active members, the more it can develop its activities within the framework of its mission. It is hard for a group to be open, to allow others to become members. In many cities, "forums of the associations" are formed, and this is a fine experience that allows people who are looking for some commitments to find a way that responds to their abilities and aspirations.

The rapid development of the first Conference of charity wound up, inevitably but sadly, in dividing into several groups that kept the name that sometimes surprises us today, a Conference. This was indispensable. The director of any group knows that it is impossible to manage a meeting of more than one hundred participants. And on 31 December 1834 — in those days people came to meetings on New Year's Eve — some serious backstabbing erupted.

That famous meeting at the end of December 1834, where we discussed a

> division, where Le Taillandier was cry-
> ing, and where La Perrière and I were
> treating each other harshly, still, we
> finished by embracing others in a more
> friendly way than ever, and wished
> each other a Happy New Year for the
> next day.
>
> (LAL1)

And we reread St. Paul's exhortation in his first epistle to the Corinthians: "I urge you ... that all of you agree in what you say, and that there be no divisions among you, but that you be united in the same mind and in the same purpose. For it has been reported to me about you ... that there are rivalries among you" (1 Cor 1:10-11). But despite the crying and weeping, despite the outbursts and the sadness, we know that we should be able to be reconciled, even, and especially when we have a common goal: the defense of the defenseless. Genuine friendship allows these divergences and animosities; it especially allows even truer and more fertile recoveries.

Seen from the outside, disputes that reach groups that work for the same purpose, especially when they are Christians, are often scandalous. We are not angels. We have lived and still live in a broken society. We would like to avoid this, but considerations of all sorts (personal, political, economic, cultural, and religious) elicit misunderstandings and tensions.

Is not the separation among the churches the greatest obstacle, the greatest sin that we can commit against God? And each year, we try to approach separated Christians in that week of Christian Unity. But the road is so long, and so arduous! This prompted Frédéric to say:

> There are Christians in all camps. God scatters us among enemy flags so that there might not be in this divided society just one party, just one faction, where some mouths neither invoke nor bless God our Savior.
>
> (TOM2)

Frédéric was well aware of the huge difficulty that separates us from the faith and love of Christ. Even he was the object of many attacks.

> The genuine dangers that we can face in Lyons, as well as the imaginary ones that have possibly perturbed us more; the mistrust and the "Lamennasian" anger of some, and the seemingly clerical ardor of others. My middle-of-the-road system displeases everyone and daily arouses contrary recriminations, but nonetheless I am not allowed to resign. These are my fears as a result, but also my hopes.
>
> (LAL1)

On the other hand, is this not the lot of those who refuse to remain in one spot, who reject routine, and who think that activity is neces-

sary and vital, even if it does not put an end
to questioning? The Vincentian group in Lille
that began the Frédéric Ozanam Welcome
Center experienced numerous snubbing and
pettiness, the opposition coming from those
in its own ranks who judged that we were
building too grandly. Why should beauty be
reserved just to certain social categories? We
have always affirmed that it not be the case
that because a poor person is poor, that we
have to, in addition, suggest to him (I cannot
use the term "offer") some miserable, even
unhealthy quarters. Every being has his or her
dignity that we have to respect. Catholics have
too often been accused of tending to act with
sadness. To be welcomed in a light and warm
environment is already one step taken to well-
being, to a recognition of self. No matter how
humble Frédéric was, he could also be revolted
by these remote ideas of the faith that he pro-
fessed. He must have been quite irritated when
he criticized

> ... those doctors who make pronounce-
> ments between reading a newspa-
> per and discussions at the counter,
> between the pear and cheese, people
> for whom new arrivals are always bad
> news, puritans from the countryside,
> for whom whatever reaches them from
> Paris is presumed to be perverse, irre-
> ducible doctrinaires, for whom public
> opinion is like the thirteenth article of

the Creed, people of all sorts who try to
monopolize everything.

(LAL1)

He could even show himself severe toward
his confreres. A pastor in a town with thermal
baths made a gift for the poor, but a member
of the Conference wanted to use it principally
for needy Catholics. Angry, Frédéric took the
floor, and declared firmly and violently:

> Gentlemen, if this opinion has the
> unhappy fate of prevailing, if it is not
> well understood that we serve the poor
> without distinction of their religion, I
> am going to hand over their alms to
> the Protestants and I will tell them:
> Take them; we are unworthy of your
> confidence.

(PER)

Reflection Questions

ↂ In the inevitable conflicts and misunderstandings that arise in families, and
   among friends and colleagues, what is
   my reaction? What is the one skill that
   I still need to learn to manage conflicts
   while still remaining loving and respect-
   ful of others?

ↂ If I have been involved in pettiness or
   revenge, especially recently, what can
   I do now to help restore balance and

charity? Am I able to say "I'm sorry,"
and really mean it? If not, what skills do
I need to practice to be able to grow in
this strength?

9

Social Questions

The question that divides the men of our time is no longer a matter of political forms, but rather a social question. The issue is to know who will triumph: the spirit of egoism or the spirit of sacrifice; or whether society will be either a large-scale exploitation for the good of the strongest, or a consecration of each person for the good of all, and especially for the protection of the weakest. Many men have too much and want even more; there are also many more who do not have enough, or who have nothing, and who want to take what others do not give them. Between these two types of men, a struggle is being prepared, and it promises to be terrible. On the one side is the power of gold; on the other, the power of despair.

(JAN1)

*I*n 1850, in the middle of the industrialization of the nation, the sharing of riches was unequal, not what it should have been. As a result, the working world suffered greatly. People labored on the average 5,000 hours a year (compared with 1,645 hours in 2011), and children as young as eight were put to work. Victor Hugo wrote this in 1856 in his poem *Melancholia*:

> From dawn to dusk they go, eternally repeating
> the same movements in the same prison. ...
> They seem to say to God: Our Father,
> Little as we are, see what the grown-ups are
> making us do!

Early on, Frédéric was troubled by this situation, as he mentioned in many letters that he wrote to his friends in the Conferences. From 1836, he started to alert Christians of this terrible problem:

> We have to rush in between these two opposing armies; if we cannot stop them, at least we can lessen the shock. And being young and middle-class makes it easier for us to be the mediators that our Christian identity makes incumbent on us.

(JAN1)

Today, the lack of equality is still scandalous. We cannot remain unconcerned about the miseries that surround us, and initiatives undertaken by different Conferences are moving in this direction. Frédéric essentially had in mind the challenges of financial poverty. These still exist in our days, of course, but there are others: think of the poverty of culture, relationships, psychology, etc. An internal review by the Society of St. Vincent de Paul brought to

light the activities engaged by the Vincentians
to help and support the women and men who
are suffering in their life: more than 130 of
these activities draw our attention and doubt-
lessly there are more. In all the Conferences in
France and all the continents, women and men
try day and night to reduce poverty through
hospitality centers, food pantries, helping in
meeting responsibilities, sending entire families on vacations, visiting hospitals and prisons, accompanying patients and their families
suffering from Alzheimer's, soup kitchens …
all of these answer a call from the Lord, as
Frédéric relayed:

> The same authority who proclaims
> to you that there will always be poor
> among you is the same who asks you
> to do everything so that it will not exist
> any longer.
>
> (EN)

Since 2003, the Society of St. Vincent de Paul
has been working on the agonizing problem of
loneliness, one of the poverties of our times
that touches more than just the elderly. A study
conducted by SOFRES (a French marketing
service) with the support of *La Croix* (a Catholic
daily newspaper) showed that the women suffering most from the lack of companionship are
between thirty-five and forty-nine, are alone
with children, and are victims of unemployment
and of the precarious conditions of employ-

ment. But we should not forget the many others who experience loneliness in their daily life: children coming home alone from school to an empty dwelling, unmarried farmers — the section of the population with the most suicides — priests living in isolation, artists abandoned by the public, the elderly with no hope of a little love, widows and widowers whom no one ever invites to a meal with other couples, since they are afraid of hurting them, although in fact, they would be happy with this (aren't we the ones, instead, who would be bothered?), rootless young people with no future. By means of all their tiny acts of accompaniment, discreet and barely visible in the media — in fact they fall under the media's radar — the members of the Society try to alleviate all these kinds of loneliness, to search for justice, and to bring a little love and charity.

> The social order rests on two virtues: justice and charity. But justice already supposes great love, since we have to love a person greatly to respect his rights, which border on our rights, and his liberty that troubles our liberty. Yet, while justice has limits, charity has none.
>
> (CIV)

Frédéric is an outstanding model for those who wish to follow in his footsteps, since he possessed this love of the poor to a degree rarely attained. He put himself at their service simultaneously through his intellectual, literary, and juridical knowledge, but especially through concrete activity.

> The science of satisfying reforms is learned less through books or in the courtroom than in climbing the stairs of the houses of the poor, in sitting at their bedside, in suffering the same cold as they, and in eliciting from them amid a friendly conversation the secrets of a desolate heart. When we have studied the poor in this way, in their room, in school, in the hospital, at work, in the cities and in the countryside, in all the conditions where God has placed them, then we begin to understand the elements of this tremendous problem of poverty; only at that point do we have the right to propose serious measures.
>
> (CEN)

Throughout his life, Frédéric wanted to be a mediator. He wanted to reconcile science and religion, wealth and poverty, believer and unbeliever, the one with too much and the one with nothing. He was truly an intellectual in the service of the needy, of families in difficulties, the burning apostle, as Bishop Baunard said, *"with the same desire to preach the truth and to save souls."* (BA) Until the end of his life, Frédéric sought to raise up the poor and to encourage us in our responsibility as Christians committed to a charitable mission. In one of his last letters (dated 19 July 1853, close to his death on 8 September), he wrote this to a priest, a professor of young Italians starting a Conference:

> Soon, your best young people in little groups of three or four along with a teacher are going to climb the stairs of a poor person. You will see them returning both sad and happy, sad for the evil that they have seen, but happy for the little good that they will have accomplished.
>
> (PEN2)

Reflection Questions

- ☙ Do I know any truly lonely people? Besides sparing them a moment of reflection, is there anything I can do to reach out to them? If not, what is holding me back?

- ☙ What has been my experience with loneliness in my own life? Have I overcome this? Who were those who helped and supported me, and what can I learn from their care for me?

10
Youth

God often uses weak and frail instruments to accomplish great things. When you are called to a providential mission, then both talents and defects vanish and give way to his guiding inspiration.

(COL1)

*I*n his homily for Frédéric's beatification in 1997, John Paul II offered him as an example to "all these young people gathered in large numbers in Paris" for World Youth Day. *"Frédéric experienced a call to love and thereby gave the example of a great love of God and man."* (BEAT). An extract from a letter to Fr. Pendola, teaching some students of the Tuscan bourgeoisie, summarizes exactly how to approach great poverty.

There is one thing that has not been taught them, one thing that they know only by name. They have to have seen others suffering to learn to suffer through it when suffering comes to them, sooner or later. This is sorrow, privation, need.... These young gentlemen should learn what hunger is, thirst,

the empty storeroom. They have to see
pitiful people, sick and crying children.
They have to see them and they have to
love them.

(PEN2)

One does not approach this reality through
theory; instead, it is through concrete and regular contact. This takes time, self-denial, com-
passion, and love. We need to really see in order
to approach poverty, even a little. So often we,
the young and the not-so-young, evince a great
ignorance, or even a great mistrust of those
experiencing trials: the homeless person, the
young man tossed out of his own family, the
elderly person living in great isolation, an
abandoned mother with children. The foundation of the first Conference of charity put these
principles into practice. That young team of
Sorbonne students, all born outside of Paris,
had a high concept of friendship born of action.

The closest bond, the principle of a
genuine friendship, is charity, and
charity cannot exist in the hearts of
several without spreading abroad. It is
a fire that burns out without fuel, and
the fuel of charity is good works.

(CUR1)

The French motto of the Society of St.
Vincent de Paul is "*Aimer, partager, servir*" [Love,
share, serve]. Those young people discovered
great poverty in a Paris with its narrow lanes

but no gutters or sidewalks. They could have remained unaware of these crowded and filthy neighborhoods where families survived being packed together in unhealthy rooms. They might have been able to shut their eyes, to walk past without looking. Instead, following the advice of Sister Rosalie (a Daughter of Charity, superior of a convent on rue Mouffetard), they turned to these needy persons to serve and love them. With great courage they overcame the obstacles and attempted to alleviate the miseries they were encountering. Later, having left Paris after their studies, they would discover the same realities in their birthplace. Frédéric often returned to this theme.

> I want all young people with both head and heart to assemble for some charitable work and to form themselves all over the country into a huge generous association to aid the lower classes.
>
> (FAL1)

While fostering the creation of these groups of young persons, he also wanted to increase their faith, anchored in generous activities.

> Will we then remain motionless amidst a world that suffers and groans?
>
> (FAL1)

Frédéric's work continues. Conferences of young people exist in schools. Young professionals take responsibilities in the association.

But there are still too few of them. Without a doubt, the young should be given a greater role in our different settings, and we, the older members, should go to meet them, since it is difficult to join a group that is constantly moving. The problems of studies, work, mobility, and home life (many women are working) do not support active and aggressive commitments over the long haul. Is there also perhaps some mistrust between adults and youth, a lack of communication? We live in a time of instant communication, involving moving, changing, even flitting about. People often complain that young people no longer make commitments. This is a short and easy answer, whose falsity is shown by examples of cooperation with young members in developing countries, or activities closer to home: offering help in managing one's life, providing meals, learning to read and write, reflecting in prayer, and visiting families, to name a few. Even one hour regularly devoted to a specific activity is important.

When he taught at the Sorbonne, Frédéric loved the company of young people, whether during their studies or when they were going out with their friends. They were delighted when they used to go to his home in a group full of affection and respect. One of them wrote him one day: *"Before listening to you, I did not believe.*

Even though you have not been able to preach a large number of sermons, with one of them you made me a Christian." (BA) He was not ashamed to proclaim his faith in God, and they appreciated this tremendously. We sometimes have difficulties in affirming our faith, through bashfulness or fear of proselytizing. We are too lukewarm.

Frédéric was always full of confidence in the youth, and he remained very close to them — recall that he died a young man of forty. His feelings were often those of his students and friends younger than he was. We can imagine Frédéric as austere and quiet because of the severe portraits of him that we have. He was, in fact, anxious his whole life, sometimes even depressed, but he had moments of great happiness, as recalled by one of his students. *"This intellectual had a laugh that was so free and natural, and he had such a pleasant manner of joking, and a lively approach that it was charming to find him in one of these sweet moments. We very often teased him, and he teased right back. Sometimes we provoked him. You had to understand him. He had such a youthful spirit. He was candid in his happiness, and gentle when he joked!"* (CHO) He loved to repeat this expression from St. Francis de Sales: "A saint who is sad is a sad kind of saint!" Frédéric concluded his letter to Fr. Pendola with this phrase that would encourage parents

who were worried about their children who
were far from the faith:

> You must never believe in the death of
> a young Christian soul. It is not dead,
> it is sleeping.
>
> (PEN2)

He had great optimism, often perceived
when he saw one or other young person who
had been away from the faith coming back to
God with enthusiasm and fervor. To fulfill his
great plan of the reconquest of the Catholic
faith by young Christians, Frédéric played a
major role in the establishment of the Lenten
conferences at Notre-Dame of Paris, beginning in 1835.

> The big meeting of young Catholics and
> non-Catholics this year was at Notre-
> Dame. You certainly heard about the
> conferences given by Abbé Lacordaire.
> He gave eight of them to an audience
> of about 6,000 men, without counting
> the women.
>
> (VEL1)

These Sunday gatherings during Lent continue today, and they are a meeting place for
reflection by many Christians who come to
draw nourishment for the vitality of their faith.
Frédéric would be happy to know that tens of
thousands of listeners also follow them over
the airwaves.

Reflection Questions

ଓଃ If I am young, what hope and inspiration am I taking from reflecting on Ozanam's life? What specific calls to charity and action do I sense within myself? If I am older, what hopes do I have for the youth of today? How can Frédéric's example help me to reach out and support those who are coming after me?

ଓଃ Do I perceive lukewarmness in myself concerning the sharing of my faith and convictions? Has hesitation to profess my faith held me back? If so, what can I do in the future to grow in strength?

11

We Are Like the Gobelin Weavers

We are responsible for making our own destiny here below, but we do not know exactly what it is yet, something like the Gobelin weavers working on their tapestry. They simply follow the drawing of an unknown artist, trying to match on the reverse side of the frame the threads of different colors as he indicated, but without seeing the result of their work. It is only later, when the work is done that they can look at these flowers, these paintings, these persons, these artistic marvels sprung from their hands for the enchantment of royal residences. In the same way, my friends, let us work on this earth with docility, submitting ourselves to the will of God, without seeing what we do. But he, the divine artist, sees it and knows. And when our task is completed, he will have us see the work of our life of labor and pain, and we will be in ecstasy and bless him for what he deigned to accept our weak endeavors, to place them in his eternal dwellings.

(GOB)

*T*his lovely text is taken from a discourse that Frédéric gave to young workers. It expresses his complete abandonment to confidence in God. All the actions of our life, in the inner workings of a married couple, in a family, at work, in the groups that we struggle in, in particular in the Society of St. Vincent de Paul — they all cooperate in the building up of the world. Even if he was often worried about himself, Frédéric always had confidence in Providence. We are close to the "Be not afraid!" of John Paul II. We should not fear for the morrow but should act and focus our efforts wherever the Lord sends us. He gave us many skills that he asks us to use in this world throughout our life. We should not hide behind a false modesty ("I just can't do it") to decline some responsibility, some commitment, even a tough one, in town, at work, in our volunteering.

We should never turn it down, despite the trials of all sorts that can come from outside — this is logical and understandable — but also from inside ourselves. This is more harmful and risks causing us to lay down our arms. How many Christians there are who give in to attacks coming from their companions, who — to use Frédéric's terms "with the best faith in the world — without realizing it, make proposals that upset, offend, and crush, but even (yes,

I am repeating myself) 'with the best faith in
the world.' " The Lord does not send us the
challenges that await us; quite the contrary, his
help lets us overcome them. Let us place ourselves in his presence. Even doing so will not
avoid failures and distress, but prayer and the
desire to hand ourselves over to the will of God
will help us to surmount the obstacles, to regain
our courage after unexpected heavy and painful blows, to strengthen us even more in the
face of adversity to combat it better: "Blessed
are you when they insult you and persecute
you, and utter every kind of evil against you
[falsely] because of me" (Mt 5:11). We have been
asked to apply ourselves, to fulfill our office
with the greatest possible seriousness (which
does not rule out happiness or even humor).
Do we have to know the end of the road, the
conclusion of the story?

> What good is it to know our destina-
> tion except to accomplish it? What
> good is it to see the path unless we walk
> on it? So, as long as the traveler can see
> it ten paces ahead, is that not just as
> good as if he sees the rest of the way in
> perspective?
>
> (FAL1)

Without worrying about the future, like the
birds of the field:

> We are poor folks, since we do not
> know if we will still be alive tomorrow,

but we still would like to know what we
will be doing twenty years from now.

(FAL1)

This does include a serious preparation for
the task ahead. The Lord does not ask us to
push ahead, head lowered blindly, toward the
obstacle! We would not overcome it. He advises
us instead to sit down and reflect clearly before
making some important decision, whether by
ourselves or as a group. We should act so as
to fulfill as best we can "our life of labor and
pain" as Frédéric wrote. We are not expected
to get spectacular or extraordinary results, but
simply to live with the talents that the Lord
has bestowed on us and which he asks us to
develop.

> Provided the worker know at each hour
> of the day the task imposed on him for
> the next hour, will he not certainly
> wait until the end of the work to see if
> has before his eyes the architect's plan?

(FAL1)

The preceding citations show that this question worried Frédéric. We are often fearful,
timid; we lack confidence in Providence. Let
us let the Lord act within us, without torturing
ourselves, without looking for empty excuses
about becoming involved, ignoring the help
that a neighbor, a friend, or a member of the
Conference asks of us. Let us work fervently

and humbly, sometimes even groping along, but hoping that our actions are part of God's plan. Like the Gobelin weavers, we cannot see where we are going, but rather are ready to help the Kingdom come. Let us place ourselves under his protection and accept his will. Let us not resist the Lord's appeals, but put all our energy into the service of the poor person whom we visit, each time, where he lives, or whom we find in our hospitality centers or offices.

As disciples of Frédéric Ozanam in the Society of St. Vincent de Paul, we have been invited by the Lord to get involved in the fate of a poor person in distress by acting in brotherly charity, instead of in the attitude of someone who is just there to help, and by aiding the person to rediscover his dignity and taste for living. We also have an obligation to keep from dwelling on the past.

> Charity should never look behind, but always ahead, since the number of past benefits is always quite small, and the present and future distress that it should care for are infinite.
>
> (CUR1)

Frédéric's spirituality is not disembodied, directed only toward prayer, meditation, and adoration. It was always directed toward activity, the daily activity that uncovers the face of the Lord through the face of the Other, in his worries, his problems, his sorrows, and his joys, to be able to share them, sympathize with them, and rejoice.

> Charity is a tender mother with her eyes fixed on the child that she carries at her breast; she no longer thinks of herself, and forgets her own beauty because of her love.
>
> (CUR1)

Reflection Questions

- ✂ What are the talents I have that could accomplish the most good in the society in which I live? Am I letting them languish, or do I take these gifts from the Lord seriously?

- ✂ How nervous am I about the future of my own life and labors? Where do I perceive the hand of God in all this?

12

We Give You Our Lives

Gentlemen, our age is reproached for being an age of egoism, and they say that professors are infected with this general epidemic. Still, this is where we lose our health. This is where we use up our strength. I don't complain about it. Our life, my life, belongs to you. We owe it to you until you have our last breath. As for me, gentlemen, if I die, it will be in your service.

(LAC)

*F*rédéric was a teacher by vocation. His faithfulness to the official university did not prevent him from remaining very loyal to those defending the cause of liberty of teaching. He was delighted with the opening of a Catholic university at Louvain, in Belgium. He was never afraid of advertising his faith, even in the highest circles. And everyone was satisfied with this, Christians and atheists alike.

I have never worked for human praise, but only for the service of the truth.

(BA)

When his studies were completed with important university diplomas (doctorates in law and in letters, and post-graduate in letters), Frédéric entered the competition to obtain a professorship in Lyons. In 1839 he was named professor of commercial law. The ministry of education agreed on the establishment of this position after many twists and turns, but basically because of money. This position freed him from the courthouse and from being a trial attorney, which he never liked at all. *I am not getting used to the atmosphere of squabbling.* (LAL1) His father wanted him to become "an upright and enlightened magistrate." When his father died, on 12 May 1837, Frédéric felt freed from this moral constraint. The responsibility of being a professor brought more than the rare pleadings that he delivered during several months at the bar in Lyons.

This nomination was one of the final joys offered to his mother, whose health was weak from several pregnancies. As she died on 14 October 1839, she would not hear her son give his first lecture on 16 December 1839 before more than 250 persons (students and auditors). He gave forty-seven lectures in 1839 and 1840. During his twenty-fourth lecture, he held forth on certain themes that would be with him for the rest of his life: ideas on the proletariat and on the place of the working man.

> Exploitation occurs when the boss con-
> siders the worker not as a helper but as
> a tool that he has to drag the greatest
> possible service out of at the least pos-
> sible price. Exploitation of a man by a
> man is slavery.
>
>   (DRO)

We are now in 1840, eight years before
Marx's famous *Communist Manifesto*, and just a
few years after the uprisings of the silk workers (the *canuts*) of Lyons in 1831 and 1834.
Emotions were still running high and a young
man of twenty-six needed a certain amount of
courage to use such language. For Frédéric,
the worker had a duty, namely work. He also
had a right to a salary, the price of his work.
Frédéric proclaimed that there are three ele-
ments in a worker: living expenses (what was
necessary), the education of children (interest
and paying debts), and relaxation to keep the
vital strength that one day would dry up. *"If
the worker does not have this, he would be selling his
life, he would no longer be renting it out; he would
be investing his strength in a lost cause."* (DRO) We
take all this for granted today, but it was not so
in his time. These ideas are at the origin of ele-
ments of the social teaching of the Church. But
Leo XIII's encyclical *Rerum novarum* appeared
only in 1891.

When he completed his post-graduate work
in letters, Frédéric was named assistant profes-

sor of Claude Fauriel, someone well known at the Sorbonne. With Fauriel's brutal death in 1844, Frédéric would have a taste, as often happens today, of the precarious nature of employment, since he did not know whether, as an assistant professor, he would become a professor. As always, however, he had confidence in God.

> Everyone can help me with their prayers. As for the rest, what I ask of God is that he conduct this delicate negotiation, so that I will not sacrifice in it either the duties of my state through imprudence, nor my Christian honor through timidity. After all, it could be useful for my salvation if I did not succeed.
>
> (FOI2)

It took four months of waiting, nerves, and activities for his nomination to arrive. He showed several friends that he was anxious, but then he wrote about the great happiness he was experiencing:

> It is almost humiliating to be so moved by a temporal advantage, but from the first moment this end to fears and worries, this growing security, and this feeling of peace touched Amélie and me more than I can dare express.
>
> (JJA2)

What brings Frédéric equally close to us is that he was quite sensitive about honorific titles and quite ambitious and desirous of succeeding in his professional career, no matter what. He would not disdain honors but would take the same steps as we would to get them. He taught for twelve years at the Sorbonne as professor of foreign literature. His courses were highly valued: *"No course, probably, is as faithfully followed as that of the young professor.... His eloquence is great and beautiful; it is the eloquence of the heart."* (BIS)

Frédéric carried out his professorial career like the priesthood, whether it was at the Collège Stanislas, a secondary school where he taught for some years, or at the Sorbonne. He prepared his courses with a proven conscience: *"Tiring preparations, dutiful research into the texts, knowledge gained through great effort, and then brilliant improvisation, with an attractive and colorful presentation — this was Ozanam's teaching. It is rare to join in the same degree the two merits of a professor, both matter and form, knowledge and eloquence. He prepared his lectures like a Benedictine, and delivered them like an orator."* (DEB)

He did not appreciate the attitude of certain sectarian students toward professors, whose ideas they challenged and whose courses they disturbed. Frédéric resolved to do everything he could to keep from having a separation of his cause from that of M. Lenormant, whose convictions he shared. He even attended his

lectures when they were being disrupted.
Frédéric indignantly addressed the disturb-
ers, summoning them back to that same liberty that others gave them, insisting that they
respect it in the conscience of others. Do we
have, or could we have, the same courage to
defend those who are attacked? He loved this
Sorbonne with a passion. A few months before
his death, he recalled:

> Oh, poor Sorbonne, how many times
> have I returned in spirit to your dark
> walls, to your cold but studious court-
> yard, in your smoky classrooms, only
> to see them filled with happy young
> persons. Dear friend, after the infinite
> consolations that a Catholic finds at
> the foot of the altars, after the joys of
> family life, I know of no greater hap-
> piness than to speak to young people
> who have intelligence and a good heart.
>
> (BEN2)

Reflection Questions

cs Am I alert to the poverty or distress that
exists in the society in which I live? Am
I like the Old Testament idols with eyes
that do not see, ears that do not hear?
What can I do concretely to be more
open to the trials of others?

cs How do I show my life commitments?
Is my principal care my own life and

future? If so, do I experience any call
from my reflection on Ozanam's life to
reach outside myself? How can I make
selfishness a thing of the past in my life?

13

Blessed Frédéric

> O Blessed Mother, how God has rewarded the humility of his servant! And, besides, from this poor house in Nazareth, where you dwelt with your son, how many rich dwellings he has given you.
>
> (COZ)

*L*ike Mary, God's faithful and humble servant whom He honored, the Church has wished to honor this other faithful and humble servant. John Paul II told us this again when beatifying Frédéric: *"He believed in love, the love that God has for everyone.... He went to all those who had more need of being loved than others did, those to whom the God of love could not be effectively revealed except through the love of another person."* (BEAT) Why join these two texts, the affirmation of John Paul II on the day of Frédéric's beatification in 1997, and these few lines of Frédéric during his pilgrimage to Burgos? I think that they go well together.

Yes, dressed for service (see Lk 12:35) Frédéric reached out to the poor with modesty and simplicity. He loved them, not in any paternalistic way, but in fact, through his respect for those in distress confided to his care, and whom he would visit, even during his illness. On the one hand, he was a child of God who announced the Creator to them; on the other, it was Mary, the servant of the Lord, for whom God did marvels. Piety and love for men have raised the most beautiful shrines in the world, desired and built by humble servants and by the greatest artists.

Marian devotion clearly marked Frédéric's spirituality. The Virgin Mary always had a special place in his life. From his earliest years he knew the Hail Mary, learned at the knees of his mother and his sister; he regularly prayed the rosary; he often walked up the steps to the simple shrine of Notre-Dame de Fourvière on the bluff overlooking Lyons. It would be significantly expanded in the second half of the nineteenth century. From the time of the foundation of the Society of St. Vincent de Paul, at the very time that it was placed under the patronage of St. Vincent de Paul, Frédéric endeavored to guarantee that the Virgin Mary be celebrated as its protectress and mother of God. We recall in a special way the day of the feast of the Immaculate Conception, December 8. During his travels, both on university business and for the care of his health, he visited the main sites of Christianity: the cathedrals and churches dedicated to the Virgin. In his letters he wrote descriptions that manifested both his profound knowledge of Romanesque and Gothic architecture, as well as his need for a deepening of faith.

> O Blessed Mother of Burgos, you are also Our Lady of Pisa and Milan, Our Lady of Cologne and Paris, Our Lady of Amiens and Chartres, queen of all the great Catholic cities. Truly, you are beautiful and gracious (pulchra es et decora), since a mere thought of yours brought down grace and beauty on the works of men.... This is not the work of giants but of angels, since it is so full of air and grace, all up to date.
>
> (CID)

During his final long trip in the southwest of France, he traveled with his family on pilgrimage to Betharram, a shrine visited since the fifteenth century. In this place, the piety of the people honors the Virgin with the Golden Branch: *With every fiber of my being, I am clinging to that liberating branch, to her whom we call the consolation of the afflicted and the refuge of sinners.* (MAR2)

This church is still widely visited since it is near the Marian shrine of Lourdes, where Frédéric would certainly have gone if he had lived a few more years. He would have gone as a pilgrim, a sick pilgrim (like Blessed John

Paul II in 2004), like millions of people today, perhaps in hopes of physical healing, but especially of spiritual comfort under Mary's loving glance. Like us, he would have asked for the intercession of the Virgin of Massabielle, and he would have been able to soothe his interior misery and strengthen his continual search for an ever deeper faith. His visits to churches were also the opportunity to awaken the faith in "little Marie."

> While I was out walking this morning, I saw a lovely church like those I showed you during our trip. There was a large Holy Virgin there with the little Jesus in her arms.
>
> (AME)

He placed his life under the protection of the Virgin Mary, going from Milan to Marseilles, through Lyons, Florence, Paris, Chartres, and Siena.

> How, in the city of the Blessed Virgin, could we see a work not succeed where the Blessed Virgin is its primary patron?
> (PEN2)

He always wrote, spoke, and acted as a witness of the Catholic faith. We might say that he was the witness of the Beatitudes, and that he put them into practice. He was a genuine apostle who: *"consecrated his life to the most noble of causes: truth and charity."* (POU)

He came back from Italy on 2 September 1853, but died in the company of his people near the old port of Marseilles, on September 8, the feast of the Nativity of the Virgin, unable to return to Paris as he had wished. *He was born into heaven on the very day when there was born on earth this Virgin whom he had so tenderly loved and so poetically celebrated.* (POU) Another example of Divine Providence: on the following Sunday, September 11, the first stone was laid for Notre-Dame de la Garde, so dear to the heart of the Marseillais. As John Paul II recalled at Frédéric's beatification:

> I encourage you to join forces so that, as he wished to inspire you, the poor will ever be better loved and served, and that Jesus Christ will be honored in their persons.
>
> (BEAT)

> In the choices that they will make, your holiness, Frédéric, will be particularly confirmed. And your joy will be great. What you already behold with your eyes is He who is love; may you also be a guide on every path that these young people will choose as they follow your example today.
>
> (BEAT)

Frédéric also practiced meditation, which let him interiorize our faith in the Lord, to hear his word, and to become available to him as much as possible. In this way he responded to the first commandment: You shall love the Lord your God. His availability led to an openness toward the neighbor to respond to the second commandment: You shall love your neighbor as yourself. Let us not overlook the external aspect, a life for others, help for others, the indispensable commitment of our Christian life. Frédéric feared that the intellectual aspect of things would make him forget what was essential.

> Let us not talk so much about charity. Let us do it, and visit the poor.
>
> (GAU)

> O Lord, grant that we may, following his example, fulfill the command of love to become a leaven of love in our world.
>
> (Liturgical prayer for the feast of Blessed Frédéric Ozanam, September 9)

Reflection Questions

ભ In reflecting on the two great commandments, do I find that I love God but sometimes do not love my neighbor? If so, what should I be doing to fulfill this command of the Lord?

ભ The second of these commandments calls me to love myself: what is the quality of my self-acceptance, with all my strengths and weaknesses? In accepting myself, how can I reach out with love and understanding toward others, especially the poor?

14

Providence

This is how providence acts to direct the activity of the human spirit. When winter begins, it looks like all vegetation will die. The wind sweeps away flowers and leaves, but it keeps something hidden, dry, and powdery: the seeds and all plant life are found inside. Providence takes care of this. Some of these seeds have something like wings to travel in the air. The storm takes them off, and the waters bring them along until they find land and the ray of sunlight that is needed to make them flower.

In this way, when the barbarian times and the evil seasons of human life arrive, we see that all these flowers of poetry and eloquence wither, it seems like all plant life and thought will perish. It shelters, however, in issues that seem small, dry, and arid: still, Providence takes charge. They thus cross through three or four centuries; the Word escorts them into new lands and times, until they find the place and time they need, until a man of genius takes them for cultivation. When he adds his sweat and concerns, they finally burst into life.

(CIV)

*I*f you look in dictionaries there is no lack of definitions for providence: the will of God, the supreme wisdom through which God guides all things; divine Providence. When you read Frédéric's 1,448 published letters, you will be struck by how many times this word is used. Add to that the prefaces of his books, and you will find that he was truly guided by Providence, in which he placed his complete confidence. He never hesitated to use this word, no matter whom he was talking to, Catholic or not, member of the Society of St. Vincent de Paul or not, friend or not. He grabs our attention by the fact that there is no fear of publicizing his faith. He believed with all the wealth of his heart and spirit. His parents had been for him living examples of an active faith in the service of the poor. He described his mother in this way:

> She was for me like a living image of Holy Church; she seemed to me like the most perfect expression of Providence.
>
> (REV1)

Let us take an example from Frédéric of the proclamation of our faith. In this area, we are often timid, engaging only in fine wishes. To keep from shocking others, we prefer to keep silent about our faith. In fact, we are afraid to affirm it, perhaps because we are not affirmed enough ourselves, being very far from the sacred texts that could be for us very useful on many occasions. Away with reproaching ourselves later. We are often like Peter, whom we do not know, standing near the fire in the courtyard of the high priest, on Good Friday, ready to deny our Lord. And we forget the men and women saints who never feared to express their attachment to the Lord, long and loud, even at the cost of their life. But we are weak: "I am going to help you, my God, in not disappearing in me, but I can give no guarantees in advance," an expression of Etty Hillesum, a young Dutch Jewish woman, with a profound spirituality, just before she was deported to Auschwitz.

Frédéric offers us a way that he employed to work with great determination. He was "simple" in living his Christianity and in witnessing to the name of God in all moments of his life. If we follow the example that Frédéric gives us, we will take a major step toward holiness.

> A tender love of God, an active regard toward men, a just and inflexible conscience about selves — these are the elements of a truly Christian life.
>
> (AME)

Frédéric genuinely worked under the protection of divine Providence in all the areas

of his life: attorney, professor, writer, journal-
ist, but also in his active and even radical life,
engaged in service of the most deprived and, of
course, in his married and family life. In his
writings we perceive a simple man, sensitive,
thoughtful, and humble, who brings to men all
his confidence in God. Frédéric was demand-
ing of himself; and he is the same for us. He
makes us understand clearly that there is only
one way to win the Kingdom.

> We are here below only to fulfill the
> will of Providence.
>
> (FAL1)

We should act energetically, living out the
present moment in love and knowing that God
is the only master of our future.

> We have to think as if we would leave
> this world tomorrow, and we have to
> work as if we would never leave it.
>
> (FAL1)

Frédéric often came back to the theme of
our future. He orders us not to be worried, not
to try to know the future: this in fact has only
minor importance.

> If we know what God wants to do with
> us tomorrow, is that not enough; and
> do we have to worry about what he will
> command us in ten years, because then,
> he may call us to rest.
>
> (FAL1)

We cannot believe that there would be two kinds of people: those men and women who sacrifice themselves, and those others who "just let things go." The following sentence is quite clear on this topic.

> Do you think, then, that God granted to some to die in the service of civilization and the Church, and to others the task of living with their hands in the pockets, or sleeping among the roses?
>
> (CER)

Our life has to be active, committed without torturing ourselves too much, doing the Lord's will, and working with Providence. Let us take our part of the task to be done, know that the Lord is with us, and that we can have confidence in him. Let us recall St. Matthew: "Look at the birds in the sky; they do not sow or reap, they gather nothing into barns, yet your heavenly Father feeds them. Are not you more important than they? (Mt 6:26).

Frédéric allowed himself to be guided as much as possible. He asks us to place our confidence in Providence, all the while telling us that we cannot remain in the cold, "under our comforter," careless and lazy. Providence does not imply unawareness or naiveté sometimes bordering on superstition.

He who taught us to ask for our daily
bread never advised us to petition a
guaranteed ten years of the good life.

(EN)

Frédéric wanted us to see it a little more like
this:

I have always hoped that God would
do the work, provided that we help him
in it.

(COL)

Reflection Questions

ೞ Where have I seen God's providence
active in my life? Do I sense the Lord
working in my daily life as well as in
the great matters that concern me? If so,
where has the Lord been leading me?

ೞ How worried am I about my future? Is
it easy for me to let God guide me, or
do I have to control everything? How
does this reflection on Ozanam's own
spirituality support my efforts to grow?

15

The Prayer at Pisa

Lord, are you unwilling to have a part of the sacrifice? If I sold half of my books to give the proceeds to the poor, and if I limited myself to fulfilling the duties of my job to consecrate the rest of my life to visiting the poor and teaching the apprentices and the soldiers, would you be satisfied, Lord, and would you leave me the happiness of growing old with my wife and completing the education of my child? Are you perhaps unwilling, Lord?

You do not accept these selfish offerings; you are rejecting my holocausts and my sacrifices. I am the one who is asking you. It is written at the head of the book that I am to do your will. And I said: I am coming, Lord.

(PIS)

*T*his extract from a very edifying meditation that Frédéric drew up on 23 April 1853, his fortieth birthday, shows the depth and the demands of his faith. At that difficult moment when we face the Lord, what will our attitude be? Even a holy man like Frédéric was fearful. He tried to get out of the line. He was ready to make concessions, to bargain with God to leave him in peace, and to grant him the possibility of growing old with Amélie and to watch over Marie. He was telling God: my life is not over.

He would have to speak about all that when advancing years, illness, and old age arrived, and when his life's work was accomplished. But Frédéric realized that he had to offer a greater sacrifice: to do not his own will but God's will, to give himself over entirely.

Is this passage to the Father any "easier" for a Christian than for a non-Christian? Certainly not. Fear of leaving a life that we hold on to -- despite the difficulties, the problems, the regrets – is universal. Despite the desire of wanting to finish his work on earth (his ambitions, his career, his mate, his children), did not Frédéric say:

> We are here below only to fulfill the will of Providence; that this will be accomplished daily, and that the one who dies leaving his task unfinished is just as advanced in the eyes of the supreme justice as is the person who had the leisure of completing everything.
>
> (FAL1)

Christians, we have this grace that accompanies us all through life: the communion of saints that we find in the Creed of the liturgy, in the Eucharistic prayer, in the texts of All Saints Day, those men and women who have preceded us to the Kingdom, who pray to God for us and who watch over us.

> Soon enough the time is coming when we will go to join our people, this great mass of people who have preceded us in the pathways of faith and love.
>
> (LAL1)

Frédéric lived in this very strong experience of the communion of saints. Many of his letters recall this osmosis between the living and the dead.

> Three blessed women will help me: the Virgin Mary, my mother, and my sister; but my Beatrice [Amélie, his wife, alluding to Dante's Divine Comedy] has been left for me on earth to support me with her smile and her glance, to pull me up out of my discouragements and, under her most touching image, the power of Christian love .
>
> (LAL2)

When he wrote to his friends who had just lost a loved one, his words flowed like those of an authentic believer, someone who lived intensely this communion of saints. We mentioned this in the first days of our pilgrimage of prayer. It is right to return to it, at the end of these fifteen days with Frédéric Ozanam. The presence of those women and men who have preceded us to the Father helps us overcome the greatest sorrows.

> How many times have these three survivors, in their grief and their dangers, not counted on the brothers and sisters whom they had among the angels? Oh, they are also part of the family; they come back to us sometimes through inspirations, and sometimes through unexpected assistance.
>
> (CHA2)

In the liturgy of the Mass we recall the saints, uniting in the same prayer those men and women who are still on earth to the prayer of those who already belong to the glory of Heaven. And St. Paul opens this for our reflection: "For in one Spirit, we were all baptized into one body." (1 Cor 12:13)

Frédéric was aware of his imperfections, but still throughout his life he witnessed to his faith, which was living and peaceful. He did so in the presence of his colleagues at the Sorbonne: *"All of us are the two servants of the same cause; only I have the advantage of the more ancient and thus more sacred faith."* (HAV2) To his confreres of the Society of St. Vincent de Paul: *"Let us be patient, since we are immortal."* (AIL1) To his closest friends: *"When God gave to fathers and mothers of families the power of transmitting life, he made them part of his creative and providential power."* (CIV) During his forty years of life on earth, although he could have periods of doubts, he was available to God and to men, his brothers.

Our condition as sinners makes us frightened in the face of death, but we should put our hope in Christ. Jesus, too, was frightened of death, but he accepted it through obedience as a ransom for our sins. We know that he rose again on the third day, and we believe that one day we too will rise again in glory. The Lord, all-powerful in love toward human beings, cannot abandon those who have faith in him, who often lead their lives amid hesitation and worry, but also with daring and confidence. It is not too difficult to make this invocation of Frédéric's our own:

> If in your presence, Lord, I recall my years with bitterness, it is because my sins have soiled them; but when I consider the graces that you have enriched them with I recall my years in your presence with gratitude.
>
> (PIS)

Faith means putting confidence in the Other, handing over to him our existence to enrich it and make us better. But it is so hard to accept God's will, even if we want to live with him! We have to open ourselves to welcome God's plan for us. What is needed is a strong faith to follow Frédéric's example.

I force myself to abandon myself with love to the will of God, and, I am sorry to say, more with my mouth than with my heart: volo quod vis, volo quo modo vis, volo quandiu vis, volo quia vis [I wish what you wish, I wish as you wish, I wish when you wish, I wish because you wish].

(FRA2)

Even Frédéric, then, put up some resistance to God's will. He knew, as we will certainly know, the difficulty of wishing what God wishes, as God wishes, when God wishes, and because God wishes it. Let us prepare our spirit to let us give ourselves to the Lord and say with confidence: *Thy will be done.*

Reflection Questions

℞ As I pray the Our Father, can I recite the words carefully and thoughtfully? What do I need to do to grow in the practice of attention to my prayers? Where will a reflection on "Thy will be done" lead me today?

℞ I have no knowledge of the end of my life, but what am I doing now to prepare myself to rest in the arms of the Lord when that time comes?

Also available in the
"15 Days of Prayer" series:

Saint Benedict *(André Gozier)*
978-1-56548-304-0, paper

Saint Bernadette of Lourdes *(François Vayne)*
978-1-56548-314-9, paper

Dietrich Bonhoeffer *(Matthieu Arnold)*
978-1-56548-311-8, paper

Saint Catherine of Siena *(Chantal van der Plancke and Andrè Knockaert)*
978-156548-310-1, paper

Pierre Teilhard de Chardin *(André Dupleix)*
978-0764-804908, paper

Saint Vincent de Paul *(Jean-Pierre Renouard)*
978-1-56548-357-6, paper

The Curé of Ars *(Pierre Blanc)*
978-0764-807138, paper

Saint Dominic *(Alain Quilici)*
978-0764-807169, paper

Saint Katharine Drexel *(Leo Luke Marcello)*
978-0764-809231, paper

Don Bosco *(Robert Schiele)*
978-0764-807121, paper

Saint Clare of Assisi *(Marie-France Becker)*
978-1-56548-371-2

Charles de Foucauld *(Michael Lafon)*
978-0764-804892, paper

Saint Francis de Sales *(Claude Morel)*
978-0764-805752, paper

Saint Francis of Assisi *(Thaddée Matura)*
978-1-56548-315-6, paper

Saint Jeanne Jugan *(Michel Lafon)*
978-1-56548-329-3, paper

Saint Eugene de Mazenod *(Bernard Dullier)*
978-1-56548-320-0, paper

Henri Nouwen *(Robert Waldron)*
978-1-56548-324-8, paper

Saint Martín de Porres: A Saint of the Americas *(Brian J. Pierce)*
978-0764-812163, paper

Meister Eckhart *(André Gozier)*
978-0764-806520, paper

Thomas Merton *(André Gozier)*
978-1-56548-330-9, paper

Saint Elizabeth Ann Seton *(Betty Ann McNeil)*
978-0764-808418, paper

Brother Roger of Taizé *(Sabine Laplane)*
978-1-56548-349-1, paper

Saint Teresa of Avila *(Jean Abiven)*
978-1-56548-366-8, paper

Saint Thérèse of Lisieux (Constant Tonnelier)
978-1-56548-391-0

Saint Thomas Aquinas *(André Pinet)*
978-0764-806568, paper

NEW CITY PRESS
of the Focolare
Hyde Park, New York

About New City Press of the Focolare

New City Press is one of more than 20 publishing houses sponsored by the Focolare, a movement founded by Chiara Lubich to bring about the realization of Jesus' last prayer: "that all may be one" (John 17). In view of that goal, New City Press publishes books and resources that enrich the lives of people and help all to strive toward the unity of the entire human family. We are a member of the Association of Catholic Publishers.

Further Reading

15 Days with Saint Vincent de Paul *by* Jean-Pierre Renouard, 978-1-56548-357-6, $12.95

Chiara Lubich: A Biography *by* Armando Torno, 978-1-56548-453-5, $14.95

Forgiveness *by* Joan Mueller, 978-1-56548-426-9, $7.95

Gospel in Action, 978-1-56548-486-3, $11.95

Tending the Mustard Seed *by* Dennis J. Billy, C.Ss.R., 978-1-56548-475-7, $11.95

Scan with your smart phone to join our mailing list to receive notices of our discounts and promotions or visit our website at: www.NewCityPress.com

Check out the *Living City* magazine of the Focolare:
www.livingcitymagazine.com